The
PHONE BOX
at the EDGE of the
WORLD

Laura Imai Messina has been living in Japan for the last fifteen years and works between Tokyo and Kamakura, where she lives with her Japanese husband and two children. She took a Masters in Literature at the International Christian University of Tokyo and a PhD in Comparative Literature at the Tokyo University of Foreign Studies. *The Phone Box at the Edge of the World* has been sold in over twenty-one territories.

The Phone Box at the Edge of the World was translated from the Italian by **Lucy Rand**, a teacher, editor and translator from Norfolk, UK. She has been living in the countryside of Ōita in south-west Japan for three years.

The
PHONE BOX
at the EDGE of the
WORLD

Laura Imai Messina

Translated from the Italian by Lucy Rand

**MANILLA
PRESS**

First published in Italian as *Quel che Affidiamo al Vento* in 2020 by
PIEMME

First published in Great Britain in 2020 by
MANILLA PRESS
80–81 Wimpole St, London W1G 9RE

A CIP catalogue record for this book is
available from the British Library.

Hardback ISBN: 978-1-78658-039-9
Trade Paperback ISBN: 978-1-78658-040-5

Also available as an ebook

1 3 5 7 9 10 8 6 4 2

Typeset by Palimpsest Book Production Ltd, Falkirk, Stirlingshire
Printed and bound in Great Britain by Clays Ltd, Elcograf S.p.A.

Manilla Press is an imprint of Bonnier Books UK
www.bonnierbooks.co.uk

To Ryōsuke, Sōsuke and Emilio,
To the voices that will
always be with you

A note on the language

The Hepburn Romanisation system was used for the transcription of Japanese terms, according to which vowels are read as short vowels in English (like the *a* in *cat*, *e* in *edge*, *i* in *igloo*, *o* in *octopus* and *u* in *umbrella*) unless they carry a macron (ō), which doubles the length of the vowel sound. The *g* sound is hard, like in *pig*, *f* is pronounced more like *h*, and *r* something more akin to *l*.

Following the Japanese convention, family names precede given names.

This story was inspired by a real place, in the north-east of Japan, in Iwate Prefecture.

One day, a man installed a telephone box in the garden of his house at the foot of Kujira-yama, the Mountain of the Whale, just next to the city of Ōtsuchi, one of the places worst hit by the tsunami of 11th March 2011.

Inside there is an old black telephone, disconnected, that carries voices into the wind.

Thousands of people make the pilgrimage there every year.

It is a passing of forms from one life
to another.
A concert in which
only the orchestra changes.
But the music remains, it's there.

—Mariangela Gualtieri

Awake, O north wind; and
Come thou south,
blow upon my garden,
that the spices thereof may flow out.
Let my beloved come into his garden
and eat his pleasant fruits.
[. . .]
Come with me from Lebanon, my bride . . .

—*Song of Songs 4: 16, 8*

So speak not too lovingly.

—*Kojiki*

Prologue

I N THE VAST, STEEP GARDEN of Bell Gardia, great gusts of wind lashed the plants.

The woman instinctively raised an elbow to her face, rounding her back. Then, almost immediately, she straightened up again.

She had arrived before dawn, and watched as the light came up but the sun remained hidden. She had unloaded the big sacks from the car: fifty metres of maximum-thickness plastic rolled up in a tube, cylinders of electrical tape, ten boxes of ring-shank nails to attach

1

to the ground and a hammer with a ladies' handle. At Conan, the enormous hardware store, a shop assistant had asked if she would mind showing him her hands. He just wanted to measure her grip, he said, but she had found herself frozen, unable to respond.

She hurried towards the phone box now. It looked fragile, as if it were made of candy canes and crumbling meringue. The wind was raging already; she didn't have much time.

They worked non-stop on the hill above Ōtsuchi for two hours: she – wrapping the phone box, the bench, the entrance sign and the little archway at the beginning of the path in tarpaulin – and the wind, which didn't let up for a moment. Every so often she would hug herself involuntarily, the way she had done for years whenever she felt her emotions rising up. But then she would get back on her feet, lengthen her spine and face the bank of clouds that now enshrouded the entire hill.

Only once she had finished, once she could taste the sea in her mouth, as if the world had been turned on its head, did she stop. Exhausted, she sat down on the bench, which she'd wrapped up like a silk-worm in its cocoon, feeling the weight of her boots, their soles packed with earth.

If the world were to fall now, she told herself, she would fall with it, but if there was even the slightest chance of it staying upright, she would use every last ounce of energy she had to make that happen.

The city below was still asleep. There was the odd window lit by the glow of a lamp, but most people had left their roller shutters down and secured their rain screens with wooden rods, in preparation for the approaching typhoon. Some had leaned sandbags against doors to prevent them from being ripped off their hinges by the fury of the wind and to stop the rain from flooding the rooms inside.

Yet Yui seemed oblivious to the rain and the dense blackness of the sky. She observed her work: the plastic and tape dressings she had used to protect the phone box, the wooden bench, the pathway of slabs in single file, the archway, and the signpost that read 'THE WIND PHONE'.

Everything was caked in mud and thoroughly waterlogged. If the typhoon threatened any sort of damage, she would be there, ready to hold it all in place.

Yui was untouched by the most basic truth: that fragility does not reside in things so much as in flesh. An object can be repaired or replaced, but the body cannot. Perhaps it is stronger than the soul, which once broken can remain so forever, but it is weaker than wood, lead or iron. Her refusal to acknowledge this meant that she didn't, for a single moment, perceive the danger she was in.

'It's September already,' she sighed, contemplating the darkness of the sky that was approaching from the east. *Nagatsuki* 長月, 'the month of long nights', as it used to be called. Yet she had repeated that same phrase every month: it's October already, November, December. It's April already, she had said, and then it was May, and so on; in the never-ending list of days that began on 11th March 2011.

Every week had been a struggle; every month simply hours stacked up in the attic, for a future that might never arrive.

★ ★ ★

Yui had long dark hair that was blonde at the tips, as if it were growing from the bottom up. She had stopped dying it when her mother and daughter were swallowed by the sea. Instead she got it cut a little shorter each time, until, eventually, it looked like this, a fallen halo. The colour of her hair, the contrast between the yellow and its natural black, had ended up being a sort of log of her grief. Like an advent calendar.

If she was still alive, she owed it all to that garden, to the white telephone box with the sky-blue roof and the black telephone sitting by the notebook on the ledge. Her fingers would dial a number at random, her hand would lift the receiver to her ear and her words would tumble into it. Sometimes she cried, sometimes she laughed, because life could still be funny, even after a tragedy.

Now the typhoon was almost upon her, and Yui finally noticed it.

Strong winds were common in that area, especially in the summer. They tore up the landscape, over-turned roofs and scattered tiles across the earth like seeds, and every time it happened Suzuki-san, the custodian of Bell Gardia, would protect the garden with tender loving care.

This time, however, the typhoon was supposed to be unusually destructive and Suzuki-san wouldn't be there. The rumour of his illness had spread quickly. The extent of it was unclear, but people knew he had been admitted to hospital.

If he wasn't there to defend the place, who would be?

In Yui's mind, the typhoon was a boy with a nasty glint in his eye, plotting to pour a bucket of water over another child's carefully constructed sandcastle, a child who was less experienced, more naive. The boy observed his victim from behind a rock, poised to strike.

The position of the clouds was constantly shifting, the sky moving fast and the light sliding rapidly westwards. The sun appeared momentarily, bathing her in warmth before slipping away again.

Then, all at once, the garden was entirely submerged in darkness and the wind's deafening roar, and everything around Yui was pressed flat under its fury.

Her hair inflated like Medusa's, torn into ribbons that swirled in a vortex around her head. It felt like a warning for the plants that would soon be uprooted, pulled to shreds. The scarlet *higan-bana*, the flower of Nirvana, the flower of the dead; the hydrangea that had bloomed and gone to seed again; the white inflorescence of the *fūsen-kazura*, with its green fruits that children loved to ring like bells.

Although it had become difficult to stand up, Yui had to check one last time that everything was well protected. Dragging herself along the ground and leaning into the bank of air in turns, she somehow made it to the end of the path. She double-checked the hooks she had used to secure the tarpaulin to the cabin, then pulled herself through the wind with her arms, as if swimming.

One of the paving slabs made a crunching sound under her foot, and a memory flooded Yui's mind – her daughter's voice calling the blocks of stone that covered the ditch near their house 'biscuits'.

She smiled, happy to have salvaged another one.

★ ★ ★

As children we see happiness in things. A toy train sticking out of a basket or the plastic film around a slice of cake. Or a photograph of a scene in which we are at the centre, all eyes on us.

As adults it gets more complicated. Happiness is success, work, a man or a woman. All vague, laborious things. Whether it's a word we use in relation to our lives or not, it's mostly just that, a word.

Childhood taught us something different about happiness, Yui thought, that all you needed to do was reach out your hand in the right direction and it was there to be taken.

Under the grey sludge of sky, this thirty-year-old woman stood up straight, in spite of everything. She considered how material happiness could be, and got lost in that thought like she would once get lost in books, in the stories of others that, ever since she was a young girl, had all, without exception, sounded so much nicer than her own. She wondered whether that was why she had chosen to work in radio. She was fascinated by other people's lives, getting caught up in their worlds.

For several years, Yui's image of happiness had resided in the telephone box and the heavy black object with the numbers 1 to 0 arranged in a circle on the front. With her ear pressed to the receiver, she would become absorbed in the view of the garden on that remote hillside in north-east Japan. From there she could see the glittering sea, smell the salt rising up in ripples. From there Yui would dream of talking to her daughter, whose life had ended after only three years, and her mother, who had held the little girl in her arms until the very end.

And when happiness is a thing, anything that threatens its safety is the enemy. Even if it's something impalpable like the wind, or the rain pouring down from above.

Yui would risk her hollow existence to ensure nothing bad happened to that *thing*, or to the place that had made it real.

I

chapter
one

T HE FIRST TIME SHE HEARD about it was on the
radio.

A listener called in at the end of Yui's programme
to share what had helped him recover after losing his
wife.

They had discussed the episode's main topic at
length in the editorial room before settling on it.
They all knew about her, about the deep abyss she
carried inside. But Yui had insisted that whatever
came up on the programme, she could handle it.

After all, it was precisely because she had suffered so much that she couldn't be hurt anymore.

'What has made it easier for you, following a bereavement, to get up in the morning and go to bed at night? What lifts you up when you're down?'

But the episode was much less dark than they had anticipated.

A woman from Aomori said she would cook whenever she felt sad: she made sweet and savoury tarts, macaroons, jams, small dishes like croquettes or fish grilled in soy sauce and sugar, boiled vegetables for her *bentō*; she had even bought a separate freezer so that she could preserve her creations whenever the mood struck her. She would always make sure the freezer was thoroughly defrosted in time for *Hina-matsuri*, Girls' Day, on 3rd March, the day she used to celebrate her daughter. She knew that seeing the display of dolls in the living room, the staged platform with the collection of figurines depicting the Imperial Court, would stir up an urgent desire to peel, cut and parboil. Cooking made her feel better, she said; it helped her to place her hands back on the world.

A young office worker from Aichi phoned in to say that she went to cafes to stroke dogs, cats and ferrets, especially ferrets. Just having them rub their little noses against her fingers restored some of the joy of being alive. An old man, speaking in a whisper so that his wife wouldn't hear from the bedroom, confessed that he played pachinko; a salaryman, who was mourning a break-up, had taken to drinking cups of strong cocoa and crunching on *senbei*.

Everybody smiled when a housewife from Tōkyō, a woman of around fifty who had lost her best friend in a car accident, said she had started studying French and how just changing the sound of her voice, using the husky *rrrr* sound and the complex accents on letters, made her feel like a new woman. 'I'll never learn the language, I'm truly hopeless, but you can't imagine how good it feels to say *bonjouuuurrrrr.*'

The episode's final call came in from Iwate, one of the areas affected by the 2011 disaster. The producer glanced at the sound technician, who observed Yui for a long moment and then lowered his gaze to the control panel, where it remained until the end of the call.

Like Yui's mother and daughter, it was the tsunami that had taken the listener's wife; their house was uprooted by the water, her body dragged through the debris, catalogued among the *yukue fumei*, 'whereabouts unknown', the missing. Now he was living at his son's house, far inland, where the sea was something you only saw in pictures.

'So,' the voice began, between regular inhalations on a cigarette, 'there's this phone box in a garden, on a hill in the middle of nowhere. The phone isn't connected to anything, but your voice is carried away with the wind. I'll say, *Hi, Yoko, how are you?* And I feel myself becoming the person I was before, my wife listening to me from the kitchen, busy preparing breakfast or dinner, me grumbling that the coffee's burned my tongue.

'Yesterday evening I was reading my grandson the story of *Peter Pan*, the little flying boy who loses his shadow and the girl who sews it back onto the soles of his feet. And, you know, I think that's what we're doing when we go up that hill to Suzuki-san's garden: we're trying to get our shadows back.'

Everybody in the radio suite was silent, as if, out of nowhere, an enormous foreign object had appeared in their midst.

Even Yui, usually exceptionally good at cutting off the most loquacious callers with a few carefully chosen words, didn't make a sound. She was only roused from her trance when the man coughed and the sound operator made his voice fade out. She quickly introduced the next track, and was taken aback by the title, a pure coincidence: Max Richter's 'Mrs Dalloway: In the Garden'.

Many more messages came in that night, and they kept arriving even as Yui was on the penultimate train for Shibuya and the last one for Kichijōji.

She closed her eyes, even though sleep was still far away. She went back and forth over that listener's words again and again, as if retracing her steps up and down the same street and each time discovering new details. A road sign, the name of a shop, a house. She wouldn't fall asleep until she knew the route by heart.

The next day, for the first time since her mother and daughter had died, Yui asked for two days off.

She started the car's engine after a long period of idleness, filled up with petrol and, following the instructions in the satnav, headed towards Suzuki-san's garden.

If not yet happiness, at the very least relief, was about to become a thing.

chapter

two

Playlist for that Night During Yui's Radio Programme

Fakear, 'Jonnhae Pt. 2'.
Hans Zimmer, 'Time'.
Plaid, 'Melifer'.
Agnes Obel, 'Stone'.
Sakamoto Kyū, 'Ue wo muite arukōō' [I look up
  as I walk].

The Cinematic Orchestra, 'Arrival of the Birds &
   Transformation'.
Max Richter, 'Mrs Dalloway: In the Garden'.
Vance Joy, 'Call If You Need Me'.

chapter

three

A S SHE PLAYED AROUND WITH the satnav, Yui tried desperately not to be sick.

The view of the sea had that effect on her for the first few minutes every time she saw it. As though, just by looking at it, the water would rush into her mouth, choking her. So she would quickly stuff something else in her mouth, a square of chocolate or a sweet, and within moments she would be used to the sight and the spasms would ease.

In the month following the tsunami, she had lived on a two by three metre sheet of canvas in an elementary-school gymnasium, with 120 other people. And yet she would never again feel as lonely as she had in that place.

Despite the heavy snowfall, almost unheard of in March, she would go outside as often as she could. She would squeeze through a crack in the wall of the school playground and cling to a tree that seemed firmly rooted to the earth. From there she would contemplate the ocean, now back in its correct position, and the crater of rubble it had left in its wake.

She scrutinised the water intensely; she hadn't looked at anything else for weeks. She was convinced that in there she would find the answer.

Every morning and every evening she would go to the information centre with the same query. Two names and two descriptions: the pigtails, the mid-length grey hair, the colour of a skirt, the mole on a stomach.

On her way back she would make hasty use of the school bathrooms, which were designed for children

22

aged six to eleven. She would walk up and down the corridors wallpapered in drawings and homework assignments. Then she would return to her small square of life, silenced by all the absurdity.

Some people, among the canvas sheets laid out on the linoleum floor, wouldn't stop talking. They needed to say it out loud to be sure it had really happened. Others, however, said nothing, as if they were terrified to read the next page, where they knew the tragedy would take place. They convinced themselves that if that page wasn't turned, the inevitable wouldn't happen. Others still, the ones who already knew everything, had nothing left to say. The majority were waiting, and Yui was one of them.

Depending on what you were told at the information centre, you belonged to one of two groups: those who knew and those who were waiting. Sometimes people would go on to another shelter, where they'd find the people they had been waiting for waiting for them.

There were hundreds of astonishing stories to tell. Everything, when you looked back on it, seemed like part of a plan ('If I hadn't been in bed sick . . .', 'If I'd turned right instead of left . . .', 'If I hadn't got out of the car . . .', 'If we hadn't gone home for lunch . . .').

Everybody had heard the voice of the young woman working at the city hall, one hundred metres from the sea, who hadn't taken a moment's break from broadcasting the tsunami warning through the loudspeaker, the repeated command to run up hills, climb to the highest floors of reinforced concrete buildings. Everybody knew that even she hadn't been saved.

The images on mobile phones, which people were now queuing for hours to recharge, played back the absurd spectacle of men, women and children clinging to rooftops, capsized cars, houses that – after putting up a good fight – followed their inhabitants into the water's deadly flow, whirling like the rinse cycle of a washing machine.

And then there was the fire, which nobody ever imagined could overcome the water. We were taught as children that scissors beats paper, paper beats rock, and water always beats fire, extinguishing it and saving our lives. Nobody could recall, from those childhood lessons, that time is everything, and smoke fills the lungs faster than anything else. That you can also die from flames in a tsunami, without the water ever touching you.

From the high ground that skirted the town, where she had run to that day after the first quake, Yui watched the ocean advance. It was slow, silent and bold, as if its destination was inevitable. What did the sea do, if not wash in and out again?

She was far from home, and her mother's message saying that she and Yui's daughter were nearly at their local shelter had been so reassuring that Yui had simply followed the people around her. She helped an old woman who was struggling to walk, she made herself as useful as possible, convinced as she was, deep down, that she was a survivor. For a moment she had even felt guilty for her good fortune.

Arriving at the open space on the mountainside they all looked out, as though on a balcony at the theatre. They held their phones in their hands, enlivened by an excessive faith in technology. They had looked like children again, back at the age when there was no difference between fear and excitement. But when the sea struck the land, and didn't stop until it reached the base of the mountain, there was only silence.

The scene was so surreal that, for a long time, Yui couldn't be certain of what she had witnessed.

The tsunami rose much higher than predicted, so much so that, in some cases, the term 'shelter' became a broken formula, a misspelled word; an imprecise definition that creates an equivalence between two things that are, in reality, nothing alike. That's what happened to her daughter and her mother, who, when they got to the shelter, found only death awaiting them.

Yui would wait on that sheet of two metres by three metres for a month, forgetting, at a certain point, what she was waiting for. The few objects she'd had with her at the time of the earthquake lay around her like a garland. Added to them were bottles of water, towels, cups of freeze-dried ramen, *onigiri*,

26

cereal bars, sanitary towels and energy drinks. Surrounded by these things that were getting older and older, she waited for it all to be over.

Eventually, the bodies were found and Yui stopped looking at the sea.

chapter
four

The Tōhoku Disaster According to the
Figures Released by the Website
Hinansyameibo.katata.info,
Updated on 10th January 2019

Confirmed deaths: 15,897.

Missing: 2,534.

Displaced: 53,709.

Disaster-related deaths: 3,701.

chapter

five

YUI DROVE THROUGH THE GREY streets of Ōtsuchi, the land cleared of people. It was one of the areas worst hit by the March 2011 disaster, one-tenth of the population either engulfed by the sea or burned by the fires that blazed for days.

Stripped bare by the tsunami, it now looked like an enormous dirt field, only broken up by a few rudimentary buildings, bulldozers and a handful of cars, the purpose of which was hard to imagine.

It reminded her of one of those sprawling, half-empty Buddhist cemeteries that appear all of a sudden high in the mountains.

The vertical flags that announced work in progress and the names of the construction companies busy in the area were tugged back and forth by the incessant wind.

As she drove up the coast, following the road as it expanded and narrowed tracing the natural curve of the bay, she was assailed by a doubt. What if the man on the radio had been wrong? Not so much about the existence of the place, which she had successfully found on the map, along with telephone and fax numbers, but about whether what had worked for him could work for her too?

A telephone box in a garden, a disconnected phone on which you could talk to your lost loved ones. Could something like that really console people? And what would she say to her mother anyway? What could she possibly say to her little girl? The thought alone made her dizzy.

The satnav kept giving her contradictory commands; she was now so close that it refused to give her any more solid clues. She pulled over and turned off the engine.

What if Bell Gardia was so full of people that she had to wait in line? Who didn't have dead people they would like to talk to, after all? Who didn't have unresolved issues with the other side?

Yui imagined one of those huge Chinese swimming pools, where all you can see is flesh, coloured swim caps and inflatable rubber rings. Everybody wants to get in, but nobody is able to swim; the water underneath, a figment of the imagination.

Yui was sure that she would never be able to speak on the phone if there were people waiting outside.

It would be like in the toilets at school. Are you nearly finished? How long do you need in there?

She rummaged in the plastic bag that was overflowing onto the passenger seat. She unwrapped one of the *onigiri* that she'd bought with a chocolate bar and can of coffee before leaving Tōkyō. Chewing, she examined the landscape.

It was an anonymous corner of countryside: run-down buildings, two-storey houses with the typical blue roof tiles and large gardens with storehouses, neat rows of vegetables, the odd chicken coop. To her right was the sea, shielded by the smooth curve of a hillside. Behind her, immovable, the mountain.

Immersed in that landscape, she relaxed. There was no traffic and no shops. Her fear that there would be a crowd thronging the phone box was unfounded.

Suddenly, after hours of clouds and rain, light spilled over the earth. Yui noticed rows of persimmons hanging to dry under the eaves of a house. In the rear-view mirror, she caught sight of a man leaving the house and climbing up a ladder propped against a tree with many branches. He had a pair of shears in his hand, preparing to trim it.

She thought about asking him for directions to the house of Suzuki-san, to the Wind Phone; yes, Bell Gardia, do you know it? But she faltered as she real-ised that the request would reveal her grief to the stranger. She hated the way people changed, the pity that made them smile uneasily or shrink back into cool politeness.

But then the figure of a man with a youthful face

and grey hair passed through the reflection in the wing mirror, and Yui knew that he was like her. A survivor.

She couldn't explain it, but she had glimpsed a corner of darkness in his features, a darkness she recognised. It was a place where those who had been left behind relinquished all emotions, even joy, in order to avoid suffering the pain of the others.

This man was holding a map in his hands, his cap lowered on his head, the crinkled paper flapping against his chest. He was looking around, searching for something.

In the years that followed, Yui would get to know the man well; she would carefully examine his back as it curved over the Wind Phone, the receiver pressed to his ear, the view of his body divided up into the small square panes of the telephone box.

He would bring a little bag each time he came, carried carefully by hand so that it wouldn't get squashed, containing two of the banana-and-fresh-cream special eclairs his wife had loved. In a ritual of their own creation, the two of them, Yui and

Fujita-san, would eat them together, sitting on the bench at Bell Gardia.

With the clearest of hearts they would look out to sea because, though Yui had moved to Tōkyō and kept her distance from the ocean ever since, after a year and a half of separation, she had begun to long for it again. Everyone said that: at first you hate it and then you slowly start to love it again, with the same excruciating emotion you might feel towards a son who has killed someone; in spite of everything, you'll never be able to disown him.

'Time may pass, but the memory of the people we've loved doesn't grow old. It is only we who age,' this man, who was now unfolding the map again as the wind played with his hair, would often say.

When Yui got out of her car, the air smelled overwhelmingly of salt. The sea was nearby of course, but the density with which it filled her nostrils unsettled her. She quickly locked the door, not giving herself a chance to turn back.

She approached the man, who had by now crossed the road and was about to start walking up a gentle slope. She left the sea behind her and looked upwards.

Yui felt the wind on her back, as though it were pushing her. It felt almost like a real hand resting there, gently pressing her up the path that climbed gradually towards Kujira-yama, the Mountain of the Whale.

'Excuse me!' she called out, trying to catch up with the man. Her voice was swallowed by the wind. She said it again, *sumimasen*, and this time the words held on and were carried to him.

The man turned, the map crumpling against his chest.

He smiled. In one glance he knew that she was like him, that they were there for the same reason.

chapter

six

Other Phrases Fujita-san Would Often Say

'Sleep cures all.'

'It is difficult to know yourself if you do not know others.' (Quoting Miyamoto Musashi)

'You can never find the keys when you need to go out.'

'A cappuccino is infinitely better with a sprinkling of cinnamon on top.'

'The superficial knowledge of a subject is often more harmful than absolute ignorance.' (Again, quoting Miyamoto Musashi)

Note: *The Book of Five Rings* by Miyamoto Musashi, along with Niccolò Machiavelli's *The Prince*, was Fujita-san's favourite book.

chapter

seven

FOR AROUND A YEAR YUI had a recurring dream.
Night after night she dreamed that she conceived
her daughter again.

Something inside her was suggesting that if the
baby had emerged from her womb once, she could
do it all again, repeat each step of the process and
bring her back.

For that first year of grief, rationality kept itself to
itself, curled up in a corner of her dreaming mind,
silently watching, as if it felt itself in no position to

interfere. And yet as soon as Yui woke up, it would crawl out of the nook, stand up and whisper that it was all a fantasy, that now she needed to be strong and carry on.

Even if she became pregnant again, and even if, for the sake of argument, it was with the same man, it wouldn't bring back the girl with the little scar in the middle of her forehead and freckles dusting her nose and cheeks. Even if she sacrificed the straight and pointy nose, or the painfully sharp cry that demanded Yui's undivided attention, there was no way; she wasn't coming back.

Fujita-san – who was now standing in front of her and, with an embarrassed smile, admitting that, no, he didn't have the faintest idea where the place was but it had to be around here somewhere – had also been having visions every night for months.

In his dream he was giving advice to his three-year-old daughter, who was still alive but mute. Mute since she had lost her mother. His dreaming self would give her every instruction that came into his head. He would take her little hands and, smoothing them incessantly between his palms, he would teach her the right way to do things: don't stick your chopsticks in your food, lay them down like this; put your hand over your mouth when you yawn, and say *itadakimasu* before you eat, yes, bow your head a little, just like that; always wash your hands when you get home, and, most importantly, smile with your heart, not just your mouth.

Manners, manners are important, his wife would always say when she was alive, and he agreed. He believed it even more now she was gone.

He harboured an immense faith in those words, those commands that flooded his head and would be repeated for a lifetime, sharp phrases that carried the sound of his daughter's mother's voice, her father's voice, and that would gradually break away, becoming her own.

'They were the things my wife said to our daughter. I heard them every day but I never said them myself. I left that to her, maybe because deep down I thought my role would always be marginal. But now I watch mothers in the street, in parks, at the supermarket, and I try to steal their secrets. I want to know how

43

you make a child talk, how you make them feel happy to be alive.'

'Oh, but nobody knows that!' Yui would reply instinctively later that evening, turning to look at him.

They spent the afternoon wandering around Kujira-yama, had a light dinner in the only restaurant in the area. Before Yui dropped him off at the station, they sat in the car for a good half an hour as the sunset ignited, then extinguished, its light over each thing. They drove in silence through the pitch-black of Ōtsuchi bay.

In the wake of uttering, but *nobody* knows that! Yui had found herself laughing at the anguish on Fujita-san's face. The surprise struck her immediately afterwards.

It wasn't surprise at the man's naivety. Yui knew nothing about fathers, neither as a daughter nor as a wife. She just had a feeling that certain complex things like happiness had to be taught by example rather than words. We need to possess joy in abundance before we can bestow it upon somebody else.

44

No, it was at the sound coming from her own throat that first threw, then dumbfounded, her: laughter. She was laughing.

She couldn't remember the last time she had burst into laughter, the last time she had felt light enough to allow herself that level of distraction.

If somebody who loved her had heard, they would probably have found it moving.

'Oh no?' And Fujita-san had laughed too.

chapter eight

How to Make Children Feel Happy to Be Alive

According to Mrs Kuroda, mum of Sakura (two years old) who Fujita-san met at the Kēio supermarket in Kichijōji: 'Praise them the same number of times (plus one) as you tell them off, make pancakes together on a Saturday morning, look when they say "Look".'

According to Mrs Anzai, mum of Tao-kun (three years and five months old), during a conversation with another mum at the Inokashira Park: 'Take them to the park to run around every day, hug them hard when they have a tantrum, don't take them to toy shops so you don't have to say no.'

According to Dr Imai, dad of Kōsuke (seven years old), Fujita-san's colleague: 'Read dinosaur books together, take them to the aquarium to see the fish, answer all their questions, including the embarrassing ones.'

chapter

nine

'BELL GARDIA?' THE WOMAN ASKED the two
strangers. She had a hunched back and an
apron with large pockets sewn onto each side. A
black dog sat beside her, happily chewing on something; the weight of its torso, leaning to one side,
balanced on two slender paws. 'Is that where you're
off to?'

'That's right. Is it nearby?'

The last stretch of road, the most emotional part,
was mediated by the presence of this little old woman.

She must have been over eighty and walked with one hand resting on her crooked back and the other dangling by her side.

She offered to accompany them to the entrance of the house of Suzuki-san, the custodian of Bell Gardia. 'Come,' she said with a benevolent smile, as if she were leading them to the outermost room of her home.

She was originally from Kyūshū, but it didn't much matter anymore where she was born, because she'd spent her whole life here. She'd moved in with her husband straight after their wedding; he was a fisherman, she told them. He had said this was the most beautiful place on earth and she had believed him. So they tidied up his childhood home and began a life governed by the ocean, their days cut in two because his ship would set out once it was dark and return when the sun came up.

At the beginning, she said, she'd been especially shocked by the gigantic crabs her husband brought back as gifts when he occasionally went up north, with their long gold-and-crimson legs. She thought they were terrifying creatures, their pincers like nothing she'd ever seen before. 'But they're delicious, you must try them.'

Looking out towards the sea, Yui could see the red pinheads of buoys bobbing on the water. She imagined the woman's body lengthened out, the years shaken off like dust from an old tunic, her wrinkles pulled away to the sides of her face. She imagined her, young and erect, with an extremely short fringe, as was fashionable in those days, standing in the doorway to the house, examining the ocean; a different dog at her heel and a baby in her arms, an older child gripping the hem of her *kimono*. Scouring the horizon with the anxiousness of a young wife, she would search for her husband's ship. Then she'd lift her arm. *Look*, she'd exclaim, and point her index finger at the tiny speck puncturing the expanse of water.

The old woman's kindly intrusion was perhaps to blame for Yui and Fujita-san's unpreparedness on arriving at Bell Gardia. They had devoted all of their attention to this woman and her dog, and then suddenly the garden opened up before them, like the curtain of a street theatre.

'Goodbye, good luck,' she called out over and over with her hand raised in the air. They watched her for some time, bowing repeatedly to say thank you. The woman, meanwhile, slowly made her way back down the road, the wind escorting her home.

In the school where Yui had been displaced for weeks, amidst the boxes of fruit, packages of freeze-dried food, clothing and blankets that were flowing in from all over Japan, she had examined hundreds of faces and all of them, indiscriminately, had slipped from her memory. There was just one that returned to her daily, always at the most unexpected times.

It was the face of a man, and the item he had with him.

He must have been around fifty; he was a big man, and had a lopsided mouth and enormous bulging eyes like a fish.

The man, whose name Yui never knew, held an empty blue plastic picture frame in his hand that he never put down, even when he slept. He would use it to look at the sky, the ceiling, and all the other things in the gymnasium: the mats, the piles of clothes, the people. Observing him with a curiosity she could never muster for others, Yui watched as the man seemed to create a title for each of the scenes he had captured, something she was certain nobody else had noticed. Every so often he would stop and solemnly study the view through the frame, then appear to write something down with his free hand.

In normal day-to-day life, outside that place, mad people were perhaps lonelier than the others. But here they were less so. The very things that drove sane people mad with pain somehow liberated the mad ones, made them feel less different.

Yui even had her doubts as to whether this man had really been displaced. She got the impression that the damage he had suffered hadn't been caused recently, but a long time ago, and that any news he received here wouldn't hurt him. Everybody would go to the information centre at least once a day to enquire about their family, but not him; and nobody would come to talk to him about anything other than meal pick-up times, the shower timetable, optional medical visits and exercises to improve circulation. Everybody would cry or try to restrain themselves from doing so in front of others, but not him. He had likely come just to mix with people; maybe he even had a home but felt the need to soothe his solitude.

In the evacuation centre no one second-guessed anyone else; they couldn't afford to. There was too much fear of causing more pain to people who were already hurting. But Yui remained on guard anyway: if someone had approached that man, if they had asked him the reason for that rectangular piece of blue plastic he was sharing his life with, she would have intervened. 'He's playing a game, he made a promise to his grandson,' she'd have responded. And if anyone had asked what the game was, whether his grandson was OK, if he was safe, she would've remained silent, and they wouldn't dare ask any more.

The truth, or at least Yui's theory – that simply observing the world from behind the frame was re-assuring, that everything seemed more manageable from there – wouldn't have satisfied them.

It was easier, in there, to accept mad people when you weren't sure, deep down, whether they were mad or not.

★ ★ ★

Yui, lying down at night on the canvas sheet in the gymnasium, alternated her daughter's and mother's faces, ruins of their previous life and visions of the sea with the image of that bovine man in his house, which she imagined full of knick-knacks.

In truth, she didn't know why she was so fixated on him but he returned to her constantly. Unable to sleep, Yui would project his stocky and disproportionate figure onto the high ceiling of the gym as he randomly came across a framed photo, picked it up, popped open the clips on the back and removed the print that was inside. And she would replay the subsequent scene (the one where the man brought the frame up to his face, and the room, the street, all the things overflowing from the world outside the window, became at once appealing and peaceful) over and over again. Imagining that scene was comforting.

She felt the same now, sitting on the bench at Bell Gardia, observing Fujita-san's profile divided into small squares by the wooden rods of the telephone box (one long vertical one and four short horizontal ones) that held the pieces of glass in place. Inside each square there was a piece of Fujita-san, a fraction of his arm, a slice of his leg.

She averted her gaze many times, worrying she was being indiscreet.

But Fujita-san didn't realise. He continued talking to his wife about Hana: 'She's stopped talking, yes, but I'm optimistic, and so is the paediatrician.'

It was just a matter of time, the paediatrician had said, because in children, feelings can sometimes turn into solid substances and it is quite common for these substances to get lodged in the throat. It's much less unusual than people realise.

'My mother is well. She's a very attentive grandma.'

Then there were the neighbours, the teachers at the kindergarten and Hana's friends. Ultimately, she was loved and she'd get better. It would just be nice if it happened before she started elementary school.

The square that Fujita-san's neck had been occupying suddenly became vacant. The man was bent over, occupying the lowest frame. He picked up the backpack he had put on the floor, and turned around.

She could see he was emotional but smiling. As if

to say, 'Everything's all right, it's all right, I'm all right, you can do it.'

It wasn't until a year on from that day that Yui would tell Fujita-san about the picture-frame man from the shelter. She would tell him how she too had once appeared inside that blue rectangle, and how, on that day, she had felt seen, *truly* looked at, for the first time in weeks.

It never happened again: three days later the man disappeared. Nobody said anything about him, and she didn't ask any questions.

There's nothing to say about those you know nothing of.

Nothing really matters about those you know nothing of.

Later, Yui realised she had learned another important thing in that place of confinement: that silencing a man was equivalent to erasing him forever. And so it was important to tell stories, to talk to people, to talk about people. To listen to people talking about other people. Even to speak with the dead, if it helped.

chapter

ten

The Frame Man's Frame

Dimensions: 17.5 cm x 21.5 cm.

Colour: Sky blue.

Purchased in a 100 yen shop on 6th March 2001.

Paid 105 yen, including VAT.

Made in China.

chapter

eleven

O N THE FIRST DAY, YUI preferred to sit and watch
things happen.

The garden murmured incessantly, as if the voices
from nearby villages were merging and flowing into
this swathe of land.

Yui wondered if the conversations between the old
woman who had brought them to Bell Gardia and
her dog were also roaming around here. She was sure
that in that loving relationship there were many long

discussions about the sea and the woman's children, who now lived in faraway cities.

After using the Wind Phone, Fujita-san had gone into the custodian's house and was browsing the library that had been curated at Bell Gardia over the years, with the help of various NGOs. Then he studied the calendar of monthly events that were held there.

The meeting was friendly but polite and Suzuki-san welcomed them both with great geniality.

As Fujita-san handed over his business card, the motion of bowing seemed to drag the old man's features upwards, into a smile. Yui chose to observe the exchange at a distance; she wanted to be absorbed into the figure of her travel companion, to be seen as part of him. Fujita-san might have sensed this, but he made no move to specify who Yui was or wasn't.

Suzuki-san also acknowledged her without prying, his eyes lingering for a short moment on her unusual hairstyle that, at this time, was two-thirds blonde and the rest dark. He warmly repeated 'Welcome' and invited them in.

Yui found the garden beautiful, almost movingly so. She asked if she could stay there, to sit and look at it for a few minutes alone.

'You can stay much longer than that. There's a boy coming later, perhaps in around half an hour, but he's often late. Just make sure the phone box and the space around it are free. He comes quite often. I know him well; he won't mind you being here.'

Yui nodded, struck by the familiarity with which he talked about this boy. Maybe one day he'd talk about her in the same way.

Her eyes followed the two men as they walked into the house. The building stood humbly behind the garden. It was white with black timber slats cladding the external walls. She remembered seeing something similar in a glossy book of photos of Germanic Europe.

Thousands of people, every year, went to Bell Gardia to speak to the people they had lost.

There were many like her, those left behind on 11th March 2011, people who came mostly from Ōtsuchi. But there were also those who had lost relatives to illnesses, in car accidents, older people who came to talk to parents who had disappeared in World War II, parents of children who had vanished without a trace.

'A man once told me that death is a very personal thing . . .' Suzuki-san said. 'To some extent, we try to build our lives exactly like everybody else's. But not death. Everyone reacts to death in their own way . . .'

As Yui walked slowly, careful not to tread on any of the plants, she wondered whether the man he was talking about might be the same one who had called in to her radio show.

She was surprised by the wind at Bell Gardia, which didn't come and go in gusts, like normal wind, but was constant and seemed to be blowing faster and faster by the minute.

Then it struck Yui that the function of the telephone, rather than to channel and guide voices into a single ear, was to broadcast them out onto this wind. She wondered if, perhaps, the dead people we remembered in life *here*, weren't in fact holding hands over *there*, if they had ended up getting to know each other, making new memories that the living were completely unaware of.

How could the feeling of lightness here be explained otherwise? Death, in this place, felt like a beautiful thing.

As she walked around the garden, Yui imagined those people's spirits being called out in a register; she thought of them sitting at school desks, raising their hands and making friends. Perhaps her little girl was playing with Fujita-san's wife, perhaps they were singing together. A world was emerging where it wasn't just the survivors who took care of each other, but where the dead also loved one another and carried on, getting older and eventually dying. There must be an expiry date on the soul like there is on the body.

That thought unsettled her, as if something momentous had occurred while her mind was elsewhere.

Sitting down on the stump of a tree, Yui opened out her right hand, followed by her left. She looked at them in turn. Was her little girl still walking somewhere, held up by somebody else's hands?

★　★　★

Around half an hour had passed when Yui lifted her eyes and saw a young man in school uniform. He cut across the garden confidently, heading towards the entrance of the phone box. She was moved by his slouching gait, typical of boys his age. He couldn't have been more than sixteen or seventeen.

He knocked into the archway at the start of the path with the holdall he was carrying over his shoulder, embroidered with his school's emblem. The bell jingled.

Yui saw him open the door and pick up the handset with assuredness.

She turned her back, so as not to be intrusive. She was sitting under a persimmon tree and looked up. There were a few pieces of fruit left, but otherwise all she could see was the branches spreading out in the air, expanding in all directions above her.

From that angle, the sky appeared full of cracks.

chapter
twelve

*Favourite Topics of Conversation Between
the Old Woman of Kujira-yama and her Dog*

How romantic her husband had been when they
    were young.

That time they made love in the orchid greenhouse.

Her daughter Marie, who lived in Kōbe and had
    married an engineer.

The awful neckties her daughter Marie's husband wore.

Namiki, her two-and-a-half-year-old grand-daughter, who would greet her warmly on Skype and then forget that the screen was on.

How delicious those crabs from Hakodate were, and how nostalgic she felt when she ate them.

Her son who lived in Germany and was bringing his new wife home for New Year.

chapter

thirteen

'SHE WAS CRAZY ARGUMENTATIVE, ALWAYS giving me grief,' the boy laughed, emerging from the phone box. As he walked towards Yui to let her know he was finished, Suzuki-san interrupted them from the doorway of the house. The tea was ready.

The boy was called Keita; he came from two villages away. He was in his last year of high school. He would walk there because the bus left a minute before he came out of the gym after *kendō* practice. He had lost his mother to a tumour that was discovered too late.

'My mother graduated from the University of Tōkyō, Tōdai. She was obsessed with our studying, both mine and Naoko's.'

'His younger sister,' Suzuki-san clarified. 'She's fourteen.'

'We were always arguing with Mum,' the boy continued. 'I thought she was on my back too much.'

'We're all the same,' Fujita-san laughed. 'My dad irritated me for the same reason, and I'll probably be no different with my own daughter.'

'I wish I'd been kinder,' Keita went on, 'but I just couldn't manage it. I couldn't even do it at the end, but by that point it was different. I was scared that if I was too kind, she might think I'd stopped believing she'd pull through.'

Suzuki-san moved behind them, into the kitchen; he would nod every now and then, as if he knew the story by heart.

'If she was here now, I can guarantee we'd start arguing all over again.'

The kitchen window shook and a rust-red leaf was

pressed against it. Then the wind dropped and the leaf peeled away.

'My father lets us do whatever we want. He always says, *Carefully consider all your options and then decide. I trust you,*' the boy said. 'But I don't trust myself.'

'Everything is difficult at your age,' Suzuki-san remarked.

Yui, who had been quiet the whole time, was impressed by the lucidity of their exchange. She had always imagined high-school students to be thoughtless, shallow, not this self-aware. Perhaps pain is what gives our lives depth, she pondered, regretting the thought.

'At least she can't interrupt me when I'm speaking anymore,' Keita joked.

'Do they know you come here?' Fujita-san asked. He was fiddling with his cup, tapping his fingernails on the yellow ceramic in a rhythm he would often replicate when he was deep in thought.

'Only my father knows, because I usually end up being late for dinner when I come here. I haven't told my sister though.'

71

Keita didn't admit this, but it was mainly because he wanted to be the one who told his mother about the family, because he had spoken to her less than the others when she was still around.

'Thank you, Suzuki-san,' he said abruptly, then rose from his seat. He took a crumpled plastic bag out of his holdall. 'These are for you and your wife. They got a bit squashed, sorry.'

The custodian put the little bag of snacks on the counter, thanked Keita, told him not to catch a cold ('winter's on its way') and urged him to work hard for his university entrance exams ('but don't wear yourself out!'). When the high-school student bowed to Suzuki-san and the newcomers, promising he'd come back soon, Yui's mind was already far away.

She saw him go through the door, his shoulder bag deforming his outline, and imagined the immense future that lay ahead of him, and other kids his age. She realised there was no need to hold onto the boy's voice in her memory: it was already there, in the garden of Bell Gardia, tied to the voices of so many others. It would probably always be there, brushing against his mother's, telling her about his exams and then his first lectures at university, about a girl he loved who didn't love him back, about another one who, unbeknown to him, he had turned down because she didn't look enough like her; about his first job; his wedding – how hard it was to organise; his first child, the joy coupled with the constant feeling of inadequacy on hearing himself called Dad.

His voice would also flow out into the lapping waves of all the others. The sea would wash them to the edge of the city, to where the port is.

And then?

And then the fish would swallow them, like the princes' rings in the stories Yui used to read her daughter at bedtime.

'And then?'

And then one day, in a kitchen of a kingdom not too far away, someone would cut open the stomach of a mackerel, or a yellowtail, and those words would spill out.

Yui remembered her daughter's repetitive 'And

then? Mama, and then what?' and the movement of the little girl in her pyjamas, tucked under the blankets of the futon, as she would bring her tiny hands to her belly. Yui would read the passage out loud and, right on time, she would cry out, 'Poor thing!'

Then she would resume a serious expression, her concern for the animal sincere.

Concern for the fish's sliced-open belly, from which the fortune of a queen or a king was fated to emerge.

When they were left alone, Yui went out into the garden again. She said a brief goodbye to the custodian and there, in the late autumn wind, waited for Fujita-san. They would then go to the restaurant, where they would eat the bright orange flesh of sea urchins, miso soup and rice with delicious homemade *furikake* and tell each other about their lives.

The clouds on the horizon seemed to melt, mopped up by a sweeping wind.

It had been a tranquil afternoon, and the evening was serene. Yui told Fujita-san she would like to meet his daughter, to look her in the eyes and tell her to be proud, that not many little girls could be certain they were so loved. But if she did meet her she would never have said it. Yui knew that the strongest kind of love is the kind that is taken for granted.

She also discovered that Fujita-san's given name was Takeshi, and she liked that combination of sounds immensely. From then on, as far as she could remember, she would always call him Takeshi.

They said goodbye that night with an affection that neither one deemed excessive. Both of them felt they had, somehow, been found, like two objects stuck together by chance at the bottom of a handbag.

That evening Yui drove back to Tōkyō on the empty highway. It was late by the time she slipped into the neighbourhood of Kichijōji, passing the glowing rectangular box of the *konbini* store at the side of the road, the dense cherry-blossom trees lining the wide avenue of Musashino-shi, the old people's community centre, the gym. Everything was sleeping, as if under a spell.

For the first time in two years, looking in the rear-view mirror where she could still see her daughter sitting in the child seat, Yui felt she could sing her a lullaby; that she could then turn to her left, where her mother was sitting, and tell her about the strange magic of that day that was drawing to its close.

For the first time since the day of the tsunami, she allowed herself to question the steadfastness she had imposed upon herself, her decision to cut the world in two, into the world of the living and the world of the dead.

Perhaps it doesn't do any harm, she thought, to continue talking to those who are no longer with us.

She just had to accept that her hands wouldn't feel anything, that the effort to remember was what would fill in the gaps, that the joy of love would be concentrated in giving rather than receiving.

That night, wrapped in a blanket, she opened a book of fairy tales.

She read aloud the story of the intrepid little tin soldier, the big fish that swallowed him, the long journey that brought him back to his ballerina standing on one leg, and the blazing fire they had ended up in, a little tin heart and a tiny star as black as coal.

chapter

fourteen

Keita's Phone Call to his Mother

'Hi, Mum? Are you there? It's Keita.

'Sorry I haven't been here much recently.

'I'm going to *juku* every night, and at the weekends I have special classes for the Tōdai entrance tests. It's never-ending.

'Dad told me even you thought multiple-choice questions were stupid. It's unnatural in life to have four options and only one of them be right.

'Anyway, how are you? Are you secretly eating sweets over there too? (*Laughing.*)

'I think you passed that food thing on to Naoko.

'When I do the laundry I find sweets and chocolate wrappers in her pockets. Once I found some pretzels and churros. It's not normal, in my opinion.

'Oh yeah, and Naoko's in love. Don't ask me who with, I don't know.

'You can see it all over her face though. Plus, she's less crabby than usual.

'OK, I'm going now. There's a woman walking around the garden, maybe she's waiting to come in.

'See you, I'll come back soon, I promise. (*Turning around.*)

'Oh, and feel free to eat whatever you like.'

chapter
fifteen

AFTER THAT FIRST DAY, YUI and Takeshi would
return to Bell Gardia once a month.

They would arrange to meet at the Shibuya Crossing,
in front of the Moyai statue. It was convenient for both
of them, and Yui loved being at Shibuya before dawn,
when the place was still deserted before the whole
world converged there later in the day. With the big
screens switched off and the traffic lights flashing amber,
Scramble Crossing was an unassuming place, a festival
float resting on a street corner with its lights out.

They became used to the car ride to Iwate, the departure at four in the morning, the break at a Lawson in Chiba where they would buy breakfast and a chocolate bar from which Yui would stuff a couple of squares into her mouth the moment she saw the ocean.

That's how Takeshi found out about her nausea, about the sea.

And Yui discovered that Takeshi, that one day of the month, refused to bring his mobile phone with him. He said that the journey helped him *physically*; he needed to feel the distance with his body. With the phone, he said, there was the risk of turning back time, of constantly laying the past out in front of him.

That was why Takeshi gave Yui's phone number to his mother, who looked after her granddaughter while he was gone. And so another person came to know of the existence of the Wind Phone and of that young woman who, once a month, made the long journey to Kujira-yama.

★ ★ ★

Yui and Takeshi only saw each other when they went to Bell Gardia. The place they met seemed destined to determine their trajectory in some way, and yet the distance between them kept getting smaller and smaller.

They began writing daily messages to each other.

On the evening when Yui, looking for a pair of gloves, found a wrapped present that had been for her daughter, it was Takeshi she texted. The house move had been so sudden, she had thrown everything into cardboard boxes at random as if the objects were burning her fingers. Even after two years, the new house concealed a frightening number of things she had once bought for her daughter, things she remembered her particularly liking or that were on sale and she wanted to buy, even if it was too early to give them to her: little dresses she had put to one side for her to grow into, odd figurines, comic books, skirts that, being so untidy, she had simply forgotten about. Yui felt a stabbing pain when she discovered these things, the excruciating recognition of having deprived her daughter of a small joy.

Takeshi responded to her message with kindness, as always.

He promised her that one day, when she felt ready, they would tackle the house together; the wardrobes, the cupboards, the big cardboard boxes that were still sealed from the move, faced with which Yui felt a genuine sense of dread.

In the same way, it was Yui Takeshi wrote to when, at work in the hospital, he thought he'd caught a glimpse of his wife in a patient standing with her back to the window, or when he saw her in the tense outline of a woman who cut in front of him as he was walking to work.

It was to Yui that he recounted the kindergarten teachers' concerns because his daughter wouldn't open her mouth there either – she would draw, yes, she would join in, but verbally she was absent. Nobody knew the sound of Hana's voice anymore, and he sometimes worried he was forgetting it too. So he'd taken to watching short videos he kept on his computer: Hana singing little theme tunes from cartoons or mangling the words of traditional songs; Hana confidently announcing the kind of nonsensical things that you could only get away with at that age.

Overwhelmed by nostalgia for everything he had lost and the feeling of not being up to the challenges life had set him, he would write to Yui saying simply that he was 'a bit sad', and she would understand.

Without realising, Yui and Takeshi became more and more alike.

Takeshi began to see parts of his house with fresh eyes, especially the places where he hid things he didn't want Hana to find: dangerous things, treats, things she had failed to put away and so were hidden as a punishment. He stopped buying clothes or gifts in advance. When he found something he thought she might like, he would give it to her at once.

He learned from Yui that, in principle, there was no such thing as *tomorrow*.

Yui, for her part, started going to the doctor again. After two years of subconsciously hoping that every cold would develop into pneumonia, that a neglected sore throat would cause so much pain she wouldn't be able to think about anything else, she started looking after her health again; she tried, clumsily, to take better care of herself.

Whenever she saw a scene that made her laugh or feel warm inside – a dog playing alone at the park while its owner dozed, a cart of toddlers from the kindergarten shouting at a passing train – she would take little videos. Like visual haikus to store away and re-watch on her way to work, or before going to sleep, or at any other time of the day that felt hard to deal with. Following Takeshi's example, she accumulated a modest collection of video clips, and gradually the foggy hours began to clear.

And so the Saturday night would come around, before the Sunday morning when they would be going to Bell Gardia together. A time had been agreed for Yui to push the palm of her hand on the horn to let Takeshi know she was there, in the exact same way she had done when she was younger to hurry her mother out of the house. Takeshi would get up from Moyai's plinth and walk towards a woman he wanted to know more and more about, and he would feel content, quietly happy to catch a glimpse of Yui's smiling face, her shining eyes, her small and fleshy mouth, her pointy nose and the hair that lay two-tone over her shoulders.

In fact, for both of them, the meetings were starting to feel less like two strangers gathering at one point in the world to travel to another, and more like a return.

Him returning to her. Her returning to him.

chapter

sixteen

Objects Bought for her Daughter (and never used) Found Around Yui's House

A dummy with a moustache.
A pair of pink culottes with lace-fringed pockets.
An Anpanman toy trumpet.
A Minnie Mouse cup with a bow-shaped
   handle.
Three diamanté hair clips.
A CD of Christmas songs.

A washcloth like the ones she used to bathe her
with as a newborn baby.
A romper (0–3 months).
A little pair of gloves with a floral pattern.

chapter

seventeen

IN THE CAR TO BELL Gardia they rarely listened to the radio, and certainly never to Yui's station. Takeshi always tried to listen live to the programmes she hosted and would record them when he was in the operating theatre or dealing with an emergency. In fact, he started recording all of them, just to be safe, storing Yui's voice in his archive.

He liked the firm timbre with which she orchestrated the voices of scholars, journalists and scientists, and the delicate and reassuring tone she used to guide

91

listeners who called in from all over Japan. He especially loved the way Yui managed to put people who
weren't used to speaking in public at ease.

Driving with the sea on one side and the mountains
straight ahead, they would usually listen to music.
Yui loved bossa nova, which was nostalgic for a time
she had never lived in, for a land she didn't know,
but whose melodies were so beautiful they brought
her to tears. She was convinced that nostalgia had
nothing to do with memory, that we actually feel it
most strongly for things we have never experienced.

Takeshi had grown up with Japanese rock, listening
to the likes of X Japan, Luna Sea and Glay, and every
so often he would introduce Yui to some of the more
melodic songs, like 'Forever Love' or 'Yūwaku'. Yui
would laugh, struggling to reconcile the calm in
Takeshi's voice with these songs that were made to
be screamed at the top of your lungs.

The car journeys from Tōkyō to Ōtsuchi were long.
And yet they were just the right length for their hearts
to prepare for the encounter with the garden on the

belly of Kujira-yama. The interminable hours of driving
– swapping places when Yui got tired, the background
music, the conversations and silences that filled the car,
the steady breathing of one and then the other as, in
turn, they abandoned themselves to sleep – seemed to
strengthen their nerves and their hearts.

It made them more supple, ready to withstand the
strain that would be caused by the wind of Bell
Gardia. Mile by mile they got closer to the phone
box, to the view from the garden, the boats, the
glittering sea.

If Yui had to describe this feeling, this pain, she
would say it was like the stabbing contractions that
preceded childbirth, the wonder of the process she
had experienced when her daughter was born: closing
to open again, contracting to then dilate, clamp and
hold, then spread your legs wide and push.

A total paradox, essentially, like one of those things
you only find when you've stopped looking for it.
Like love, true love, or children that won't come.

Would they be able to speak to their loved ones
that day?

Would Yui, waking up and finding herself alone in the apartment, suffer a little less that month? Would Takeshi stop staring at the empty side of the bed or hesitating outside the bathroom door wondering how long his wife would be in there for, to then whisper sweetly, 'take your time, darling'?

chapter
eighteen

Yui's Favourite Brazilian Songs, Past and Present

'Águas de Março' by Elis Regina, original version
from the album *Elis* (1972).

'Desandou' by Caio Chagas Quintet from the
album *Comprei um Sofá* (2017).

chapter

nineteen

'ALL I WANT IS ONCE, just once, for him to let me know he's there and that he hears me. That he's not angry with us.'

Something in that gentle and resigned sentence, which followed a series of ferocious ones, snapped. The man hurriedly gulped in some air, swallowed a hiccup and started up again with the accusations and insults.

They had seen him in the morning, as they were driving up towards Bell Gardia with their usual *omiyage* for Suzuki-san and his wife, and their specific hunger for the sea urchins and miso soup from the little restaurant they always went to afterwards. Takeshi had brought the two cream-and-banana special eclairs that his wife had loved so much, and Yui had her chocolate in the glove compartment.

In short, all as usual. All a return to what they'd come to know.

'I'm a writer by profession, a journalist. And if I ever write this rotten story, if my wife ever allows me to, I'll call it *The Age of Immortality*.'

They were sitting in the room across from the library, where Suzuki-san had created an informal space to talk and drink tea, a precursor to the cafe he would open later in the year.

'A powerful title,' the custodian said in a kindly tone from the little kitchen off to the side.

'The only possible title, in my opinion. I'll talk about how young people have no understanding of risk, how they're oblivious to their own mortality, to the fact that if they do stupid things, sooner or later they'll be putting their lives on the line.'

He was a robust man, with a protruding stomach and thick, square-framed glasses. Verbose and impatient, he often forgot to breathe, and would be in apnoea by the end of the sentence. But then he'd hastily fill up with air and start off again.

'Do you remember the video of those cretins who threw themselves into the river during the typhoon last year, in Hiroshima . . . those boys in their underwear on a dinghy . . . yes, a rubber dinghy, like the ones you take into the sea on holiday, the ones you put small children in and they pee themselves immediately? It was on the news.'

Yui and Takeshi looked at one another but neither could recall having seen the video.

'Well, why would you have seen it? It was a disgraceful spectacle; just imagining it would make you sick, let alone watching it from start to finish. In any case, one of those three cretins was Kengō, my son.'

The next day Yui and Takeshi would search, each on their own phone, for the NHK video clip in which two young boys, one bleach blond and the other with smoky black hair, were on a rubber dinghy in their underwear, sneering at their friend who was yelling at them from above (from the riverbank? or was it a bridge?). The shot lasted just a few seconds because they were quickly dragged away by the current, out of the frame, and it stopped there. The NHK video replayed the sequence three or four times, alternating it with panoramas of the river and the damage the typhoon had caused to houses in the area. The journalist's voice, aided by subtitles, recounted the details of how it ended: after four hours of combing the riverbed (prolonged by the adverse weather conditions), an underwater video camera was lowered and eventually they were found.

'The boys were floppy as rags,' the man said. 'Fish were nibbling at them. There was even a crab in Kengō's hair.'

Takeshi and Yui, who until then had only sent text messages to each other, that night decided to speak on the phone for the first time. They were both distressed, imagining, above all, the number of times (tens? hundreds?) the father must have replayed that clip, alternating between desperation, shock, maybe rage, and a superhuman effort to console himself with the idea that, at the end of the day, the boy had at least been having fun.

'An idiot, a true idiot. How on earth did he think he'd get away with it?' the man had resumed. The fact that his friend had drowned, too, he added, had helped him to accept his son's death, as had the third one's suicide. Not because he would ever wish such a thing upon the other boys, but because each of the three families could thus exonerate themselves of having brought up their children the wrong way.

This man and his wife, extremely strict, had laid a road paved with 'nos' in front of Kengō. The parents of Kōta – the friend who drowned with him – on the contrary, had been permissive, convinced that if they always said 'yes', the boy would work out exactly what he wanted, without inventing conflicts for himself. And then there was the third, Katsuhiro – his personality the complete opposite of Kengō's and Kōta's – who hadn't been able to bear the guilt of having survived. He hadn't tried to stop his friends; in fact he had pushed them to venture further.

'The fact that all three of them died, though at

different times, convinced us that however we'd behaved, it would've ended up like this. That sometimes, to cross over to the other side, you just have to be unlucky.'

The man, full of scorn, repeated the sentence: 'One stupid stunt is enough, just one. And everyone pulls in some way or other when they're young . . .'

Bad luck. All it took was a stroke of bad luck. He had been a cretin when he was young too. And them? Of course Yui and Takeshi had done foolish things, hadn't they? And it all turned out OK, didn't it? There. It was luck, pure luck.

'I felt ashamed to tell the truth for a while. People come here to Bell Gardia crying for people who have died despite themselves, people who did everything they could to avoid dangerous situations. But that's how chance works, and life is a game of chance.'

There could have been space here for words of comfort and consolation, but the man couldn't handle the silence, and neither Suzuki-san, Yui nor Takeshi had time to formulate the right words.

'I pour all of these thoughts into that receiver, and

many more,' he took off again. 'I don't censor myself in the slightest. I tell him he was an idiot. I talk and talk and nothing comes back, just silence. But then, in the night, and I know it sounds absurd, I dream, and he responds to everything I've said, blow by blow. It sounds like the lines of a script cut in half.'

Yui believed him; she remembered her own dream, the one she'd had for an entire year, where she reconceived her daughter. Takeshi also recalled the lessons he had given Hana in his sleep, so it didn't take much for him to understand the man either.

'I know it's illogical. I've never remembered a dream in my whole life. But that's how I converse with my son now, in my dreams. Well, it's not exactly conversing. Each of us says his part, in turn. That way we don't argue at least, and we have time to think about what to say back.'

Behind the counter, Suzuki-san dried his hands. He brought the kettle of boiling water to the table and told the man that whatever form conversation takes, it is a wonderful thing.

'Today, for example,' the man went on, 'I told him

his mother had found a drawing pad from when he was in elementary school.'

He took his phone out of his bag and found the photo.

In the centre of the picture was a crayon drawing of Kengō as a child, stretching out his arms right to the edges of the page. And everybody was inside that extraordinary embrace, the man said, even the house, even the planet, which he had drawn smaller than his own face, in blue.

His wife had stuck the drawing up in the kitchen, in a place where she could look at it while she made dinner, and where he, walking past, would feel soothed. Whenever he looked at it, he said, he felt like a father again.

'We're still parents, even when our children are no longer here.'

chapter

twenty

Two Things Yui Discovered from Googling 'Hug' the Next Day

As part of a study conducted by the Kyōto Advanced Telecommunications Research Institute International (ATR), an unspecified number of people were asked to have brief fifteen-minute conversations with their partners. At the end of the meeting, some of the participants were told to hug. The research found a significant decrease in cortisol levels (the stress hormone) in the blood of the subjects who had been hugged compared to those who hadn't.

A famous citation from the American psychotherapist Virginia Satir (1916–1988) reads: 'We need four hugs a day for survival. We need eight hugs a day for maintenance. And we need twelve hugs a day for growth.'

chapter

twenty-one

THAT DAY, ON THE JOURNEY home, Takeshi was more talkative than usual. The man's story had really affected him. He had noticed severe psoriasis on his elbows, all his fingers and behind his ears, which he scratched at regular intervals. He internally diagnosed him with a neurosis that would require a long course of treatment.

Yui, at the wheel, remained silent.

When night fell, the landscape seen from the car became a single mass of darkness dirtied by the ugly smears of headlights and street lamps. Yui didn't like looking at it. The glare from vehicles hurtling in the opposite direction made her tense.

Takeshi said he would never be able to listen to other people's stories like Suzuki-san did. Once a month was one thing; it was quite another to do it every day.

As they came out of a tunnel, the road stretched away through a wide valley. Yui directed her gaze into the distance, up to the mountains that rose steeply to their right and left.

'You know the thing about the hug?' Takeshi said. 'That guy's son's drawing . . .'

Yui nodded, her eyes on the road.

'Hana pretends to be asleep when she wants a hug.'

Yui turned to look at Takeshi for a moment. Long enough for him to understand that she was listening.

'She does it when she's tired, or a bit sad. She's done it ever since she was tiny and really believed that if she closed her eyes nobody would be able to see her.'

How many things a hug can fix, Yui wondered. It can even realign your bones.

'Does she not let you hug her when she's awake?' she asked.

'She does, but she's a bit shy about it. As if she's embarrassed that she needs it.'

In a flash, Yui felt her own daughter's little arms wrapped around her legs, her joyful grip not letting her move. *I'm going to fall*, she would say. *Be careful!* She had to stay quiet to stem her tears.

Recently the pain of others had become quieter to her. She still suffered, she didn't like it, but it didn't deafen her either. She knew that was a good thing, deep down.

'And so I wait for her to fall asleep, or pretend to fall asleep, and then I hug her,' Takeshi said as they passed under the sign that informed them they were crossing from Saitama into Chiba. 'I've also told my mother to do it when they're together. She's not a very physical person, she wasn't with me even when I was a child, but I think she likes it too.'

'You're doing the right thing. A person can never have too many hugs,' Yui said, and immediately thought about how often, in reality, banality coincided with the truth.

'I've always thought the best hugs are the ones you give without anyone realising, just for the sake of it. Ones given selfishly, just for you.'

'What do you mean?'

'I used to do it with Akiko, my wife, you see, when I had night shift after night shift in A & E, and I wouldn't get home until after she had gone to bed. She'd be angry, she was sad, sometimes we'd argue in the morning and she would say she felt as if she'd married me just to spend time alone. Sometimes she was so angry she would burn the breakfast on purpose,' Takeshi said, laughing. 'Maybe she hoped I would complain so that we could argue more, but I wouldn't say anything.'

'Burn it?'

'Yep, actually burn it! The fish would be black on one side, and the toast was like charcoal,' he said. 'You know, it might sound strange, but on the nights when I held her in her sleep, I mean without waking her up, when I hugged her just because I wanted to, we'd greet each other in the morning and she'd be in a good mood. She was happier; we wouldn't argue.'

'And the toast?'

'Decisively less burned!'

It was almost morning by the time they got back into Tōkyō. Takeshi and Yui agreed that the things you end up missing most about somebody when they're gone are their flaws: the most ridiculous or annoying things.

'I wonder,' said Takeshi, 'whether it's because you had such a hard time accepting those things at first that now it's impossible to forget them. It's like every time they do something that irritates you, you try to balance it out with the positive things about them. It's a bit like repeating in your head each time, *I love this person because . . .*'

chapter
twenty-two

*(1) Akiko's Punishments When Takeshi Came
Home Late and (2) Akiko's Techniques for
Making Peace with him Afterwards*

1. Burn his breakfast, hide his house keys, dress
   particularly attractively and, on leaving, deny him
   a kiss at the door.
2. Bump into him around the house, pretend to be
   asleep and let him hug her, burn his toast and exclaim,
   laughing, 'Oh I'm sorry, it's just a little bit burned!'

chapter

twenty-three

YUI HAD NEVER BEEN INSIDE the telephone box
at Bell Gardia. But every time she was there, she
would imagine going in. In fact, if someone had
asked her to, she'd have been able to conjure up a
clear image of herself standing behind the glass with
the receiver pressed to her ear.

In reality though, Yui would just wander around
the garden, while Takeshi (who did make use of the
phone) told his wife what had happened in the last

month and what he and Hana had planned for the next one.

They would get to Bell Gardia at around eleven in the morning, park at the edge of the property and say hello to Suzuki-san, who was usually walking down the driveway to greet them. Takeshi always seemed desperate to talk to his wife, as if their long journey would only truly be over once he had picked up the receiver. Suzuki-san must have sensed his restlessness too as, after the first couple of times, he stopped inviting them in for tea. 'See you later,' he'd say. 'I'll be in the house.' And he would go back inside.

Takeshi would hurry over to the telephone box and close the door behind him. Yui would wait for him on the bench a few metres away, watching as he bent over the receiver and dialled a number that only he knew.

Sitting there, Yui memorised every detail in the frames that divided up Takeshi's body. His erect posture, his long legs and angular knees. The many moles peppering his arms, only revealed in the

116

summer when he wore short-sleeved shirts. Tufts of his thick, grey hair appearing in the highest squares, and his jovial eyes in the row below. But of all the segments, her favourite was the middle right one, where she could see the fingers of his free hand rhythmically drumming the shelf. She always wondered what music was playing in his head.

As time went on she began to notice herself feeling tender towards the shape of this man. Yet, each time, she stopped herself from feeling anything more.

When Takeshi was finished, they would go into the house and, if Suzuki-san didn't have anything urgent to do, they'd drink a cup of mint tea or *hōjicha* together, or eat one of the banana-shaped cakes they always brought as a gift from Tōkyō. They'd talk about the events he was holding in the library, the emails he had received, publications that were coming out inspired by the magic of Bell Gardia.

'A professor at Harvard is including the Wind Phone in a clinical psychology course.'

'Really?'

'Indeed, and apparently he might come and visit

Bell Gardia next summer. He'd like to write a long article in an American magazine.'

'Congratulations, Suzuki-san, what an honour!'

'That's wonderful news!'

At one point in the middle of the conversation, Yui became silent and left the room with a small bow. She wanted some time to walk around the garden on her own and, although nobody said a word, they all hoped today might be the day.

But Yui only weaved in and out between the flowers and plants. She let the wind caress her and almost drag her along; like a puppy on a lead, pulling just to burn off the excess joy of being in the world.

Yui still didn't feel strong enough to go into the phone box and talk to her mother and daughter. Just standing on the threshold drained any courage she might have had. She was still alive, despite herself; even without them, she was surviving.

On the trains in Tōkyō, changing between one line and another, she sometimes put conversations together, questions to ask her daughter; she would come out of the radio station and imagine telling her mother how the recording had gone, about the expert who wouldn't stop saying 'therefore' or about the caller who sounded as if he was on the toilet. Light-hearted things, like about a new colleague who had invited her out but she'd said no. He's nice, Mum, quite attractive, but there's something missing, I don't know, a certain complexity; I don't think he'd be able to understand me, truly.

But then she would replay the last time she had seen her mother. In the morning, when she dropped her daughter off in a hurry because she had to get to the other side of the city to renew her driving licence. The little girl had a fever so she couldn't go to kindergarten.

She remembered what clothes her daughter had on, because she had got her dressed. But her mother – what was she wearing? What had she picked out of her wardrobe that morning?

If the Wind Phone had been available during the weeks Yui was living in the school gym, she probably would have asked her, 'What did you put on that morning, Mum? Were you wearing a skirt or trousers? What colour? Any pattern? I need to know. I need to tell the police, so that they'll recognise you straight away when they find you. We can't let too much time pass, because your documents are in your handbag, and I have no idea where that is.'

Every time they passed Ōtsuchi and began the climb up to Bell Gardia, Takeshi tried to encourage her: 'Do you want to go in first?' But Yui would just smile and lower her eyes.

She'd head off at her usual meditative pace, roaming the garden, enveloped by the wind.

After a year had passed, Yui began to wonder whether she'd ever do it. Whether she'd ever be able to lift the receiver and speak into the wind.

chapter
twenty-four

What Yui's Mother and Daughter Were
Wearing on the Morning of 11th March
2011

Yui's mother: a beige jacket with a belt tied around the waist, a pair of black trousers, a white blouse with a light tan-and-white striped V-neck pullover, black moccasins with tassels, a necklace with an inscription of Yui's name.

Yui's daughter: a little green skirt with black leggings, a white jumper with a small bear on the right-hand pocket and the same bear on the back with its paws covering its eyes, a pair of Hungry Caterpillar socks, pink-and-white trainers with a strip that flashed as she walked.

chapter

twenty-five

A S THE MONTHS PASSED, THE two of them and the custodian of Bell Gardia got to know each other well. Suzuki-san learned each of their stories, memorising the details of their lives: they both lived in Tōkyō, she worked on the radio, he was a surgeon. He had a three-year-old daughter and a mother, she had nobody anymore. He was thirty-five, she thirty-one. They had met there, and had become friends. They would come once a month, then twice a year for the next thirty years, even once he was no longer around. After around ten months Suzuki-san sensed that they were falling in love, but he didn't tell anyone. He would often reiterate to his wife: 'Love is like therapy, it only works when you believe in it.'

'But most importantly,' she would echo, 'it only works when you're ready to work at it.'

Yui and Takeshi tried to participate in the initiatives and events that took place at Bell Gardia, as long as they coincided with the days they had planned to go. They contributed small amounts to the collection of funds for seminars that doctors and therapists from all over Japan would attend. On those occasions, managing grief was transformed into something that could enrich entire communities. Yui would mention these meetings on the radio. She was convinced that Bell Gardia *worked*, and that others, like her, would be able to find a bit of comfort on that hillside above Ōtsuchi.

Yui and Takeshi gradually realised that the Wind Phone was like a verb that conjugated differently for each person: everybody's grief looked the same at first but was, ultimately, unique.

There was one young boy who went to Bell Gardia every evening to read the newspaper out loud to his grandfather. There were many who went there to cry and nothing more. One went to console a dead relative who hadn't been buried, who was lost, God knows where, at the bottom of the ocean or in one of the many piles of bones created by the war. There was a mother who had lost three children in the tsunami and couldn't bear the silence, so she talked and talked, trying to fill the void that remained. There was a little girl who would phone her dog, asking him what the afterlife was like; an elementary-school student who wanted to say hello to his classmate who, even though he was still alive, he hadn't seen since the boy's parents had had to go back to China. He missed playing with him.

It was easier to begin to understand how people worked when you spent time at Bell Gardia.

But not all dead people were missed. There were people who hated their dead relatives and couldn't stand the idea that their punishment was over, just like that. Some people felt that death was a lucky escape; they thought, *Thanks a lot, you've slipped away leaving this mess behind and now I have to carry the burden of all your mistakes.* Suicides, for example; it was rare for people to entirely forgive them. The wives their husbands, the husbands their wives. The children, especially when they were young, were the fiercest.

Takeshi was convinced that it was the survivors, the people left behind, who gave death a face. That without them, death would be nothing more than an ugly word. Ugly but, deep down, harmless.

Yui developed her own theory: that for some people, life started loosening their joints when they were still in the cradle, and they had to work hard to hold the pieces together. She imagined those people juggling a bundle of limbs, ears, feet and kidneys in their arms, like parts of the game Operation. But then, at some point, something would slot into place: they'd fall in love, start a family, get a well-paid job, a nice career and they would begin to feel more stable. The truth was, though, they were just giving out parts of themselves to relatives and trusted friends; they were learning that it was normal not to be able to cope on your own, and that asking people for help was the only way forward if there were other things they wanted to do with their lives. They had to depend on others.

And then? Then what would happen? That's where Yui believed luck came into it. Because if those people lost someone who had been looking after a fundamental piece of them, they would never be able to regain their balance. The harmony would be gone, along with their loved one.

Yui believed she was the perfect example of that kind of person. And that, before they died, her mother had carried one of her intestines, and her daughter a lung, and for that reason, however much happiness she experienced, she would always struggle to eat and to breathe.

But she was wrong. And if she had said it out loud, Takeshi would have told her the truth.

That love is a miracle. Even the second time round, even when it comes to you by mistake.

chapter

twenty-six

*Parts of Yui's Body she Entrusted to Others
Over the Years*

The little finger of her right hand to the girl who
   sat next to her in elementary school
                           (returned in one piece after six years)

Her left foot to her best friend at junior high
   school, to which she added her right foot and

129

both legs when they moved from junior high to
high school

>*(returned when the friend*
>*moved to the United States)*

Her right breast, bladder and the inside of both
cheeks to her daughter's father

>*(left to languish, and, suffering*
>*from their absence, reclaimed)*

Her spine to the editorial staff of the radio where
she worked

>*(still on consignment)*

Her heart to her father

>*(returned crumpled up when he*
>*remarried; it took years to heal — she*
>*would entrust nothing more to him)*

chapter

twenty-seven

WHEN SHIO FIRST STARTED READING his father's
Bible he found only names. An uninterrupted
string of names, which when read out loud seemed
like nothing more than sounds. It was a list of all the
humans in the world, he told himself, those who
already existed as well as the ones who would, one
day, be here. He didn't think a list of numbers could
ever be as powerful as that.

Most people would find the Bible mind-numbingly
dull. But Shio was won over by the poetry in those

words. He would whisper them in the bathroom, the place he'd go whenever he needed some peace, some time to think. By uttering the words, over and over again, they turned into magic spells.

They reminded him, somehow, of a bed of seaweed in an ocean so thick with it that it was difficult to walk through. Escaping from conversations, he would sit on the toilet reciting half a page at a time and imagine his feet submerged in the most nauseating goop, which was, to him, what seaweed felt like.

He would never become a fisherman like his dad. And he was certain that this fact, which had come to light naturally when he was a child, was the first great disappointment of his father's life.

The Bible spoke about shepherds and fishermen, about animals guided through valleys by a dog and a stick, and about the miracle of pulling up a net and finding fish inside it. Shio wondered if that was why his father loved the Bible so much, because, somehow, he saw himself in it: a fisherman not of fish, but of kelp.

★ ★ ★

Ever since he was a child, Shio's teeth tingled whenever he touched seaweed. He shuddered with disgust when he was forced to get into the sea and walk out to his father's boat, feeling it wrapping itself around his calves, or when his friends dared him to swim off the beach and he'd have to wade through it in the first few metres of water. He much preferred to jump in off the rocks, risking getting smashed to pieces just to avoid being touched by that repugnant mass. He had to keep telling himself that it wouldn't be long before he'd be out in the open sea, and, on his return, that he'd soon be back on the beach.

He hated it. It reeked of fish but it wasn't fish, the colour made it look rotten and diseased, the texture was *snotty*, as he used to say when he was a child. The flavour was revolting too. His younger brother, when he wanted to get revenge for something, would throw it at him, knowing exactly what Shio's weak point was.

And yet to his father seaweed was everything. Every day in his boat he collected it, pulled it to the shore and, spreading it out like laundry over the long rods on the beach, left it to dry. Shio's mother and his sisters did the rest: the seaweed was dried, carefully packaged and sent off to shops and markets all over Japan.

After the loss of his father, Shio tried hard to make himself like it, but he couldn't. He devoted himself wholly to the task, even offering to take his father's place on the boat, to go out harvesting. Habit is a remedy, people would say; you can get used to anything if you do it enough.

It took him less than a week to understand that this may be true, you really could get used to anything, but also that life deteriorated when spent in the proximity of something you hated that much. It was exhausting; it wasn't worth it.

He decided to pursue a different path. Rather than becoming a fisherman he would study medicine. But, out of respect for his father, he swore that he would learn, by heart, the mysterious book that lay on his father's bedside table. The book his father had read every day, without fail, for years: the Holy Bible.

Shio wasn't a believer; he never would be. And

perhaps his father wasn't either. But he was convinced that the man had approached that book like a sort of manual, life lessons from a faraway culture, so distant that he might never understand it fully. It was beautiful though, breathtakingly so.

Shio would leaf through the worn pages, point his finger at random and begin to recite the infinite list of names, numbers and stories. And every time he did so, he would think about his father, about the absurd way he had died.

On the day of the March 2011 earthquake, off the coast of Ōtsuchi, the earth's crust shook violently. Like a rug pushed into a wall, the sea rose and fell in vertiginous ridges and Shio's father's boat was tossed onto the shore. But the shore was no longer there.

Atop the terrifying mass of water, he reached the town, soaring over the streets he had cycled down that very morning, buildings he had been in and out of over the years, places he had lived or where people he knew had worked; the old dentist who had looked after his cavities since he was a boy, the barber who always gently massaged his head after shampooing.

The boat transgressed every reasonable boundary and was marooned on the top of a building that had been gutted by the detritus and water. And there it remained.

The boat was miraculously unscathed. And yet, inside it, his father, at some point on that turbulent journey from the sea onto the land, had been sliced in two.

Yui and Takeshi met Shio in the summer of their second year visiting Bell Gardia.

He was a slim young man with a focused and intelligent face. He kept his head shaved, for practical reasons, and always wore a face mask hooked over his small ears. He would only reveal his whole face when he brought his teacup to his lips, and then they would see his broken front tooth and the hint of worry that pulled at the corners of his mouth. He seemed inseparable from his shoulder bag, which they would soon discover contained his father's old Bible.

Shio had been travelling to the phone box at Bell Gardia to talk to his father for three and a half years. He went every two or three weeks, and his visits often coincided with Yui and Takeshi's trips there from Tōkyō.

He spent most of his afternoons and evenings at the hospital where he was an intern, but he would set aside two hours on a Sunday morning to visit the Wind Phone, each time finding himself more aware of – and angry about – what had happened.

Suzuki-san knew Shio's routine from memory and would follow him with his eyes as he did two laps of the garden on foot, losing himself in the view of the sea, among the bluebells in summer and the *higan-bana* in early autumn. Like Yui, Shio loved to study the flight of the dragonflies riding on the wind on August and September days at Bell Gardia and, filling his lungs with salty air, he would count the flowers, reciting a rhyme from his childhood.

Those short walks reminded him of the books of pressed flowers he used to compile with his mother, the leaves she slid between the pages of whichever book she was reading or had in her bag at the time.

Still now, if he opened any volume on the bookshelf at home, he would likely find a pressed violet or the five rust-red fingers of a *momiji* leaf.

Shio especially loved watching the boats docked in the port from up there. On days when the sea was particularly choppy, he enjoyed seeing their bows rearing up, then plunging back down again. It looked as though they were constantly nodding, like the nurses trying to reassure elderly patients at the hospital but never really listening to them. *Yes, yes, you're right. Yes, yes. Anyway, here's what we'll do. Now let's stand up, give me your arm, now open your mouth, that's it.* Shio found this method profoundly sad, as if it were age that determined relationships between people, rather than personality.

And there were the numbers again. Everyone in the hospital was reduced to names and numbers, like in the genealogies of the Bible. In those moments he doubted whether he was cut out to spend his whole life working there.

One Sunday morning, when they both happened to be at Bell Gardia, he mentioned this to Takeshi, who nodded sympathetically. Exactly the same thing happened in Tōkyō; it wasn't a provincial thing. In fact, people probably cared more in the hospital where Shio worked, because they knew each other better. The busier it was, unfortunately, the more difficult it became to treat people as individuals. To be honest, paying special attention to each patient would break up a nurse's routine, and, in the long run, if you didn't have a routine, you risked getting burned out.

Yui thought Shio was brilliant, gifted with a rare sensitivity. Takeshi caught in him a reflection of himself in the early days of his career, when he was working in the accident and emergency department. Skipping from one patient to another and going home with his back almost broken from two hours of sleep on a camp bed, had felt to him like the closest thing to serving humanity.

They became friends. Takeshi always tried to dedicate at least an hour to listening to Shio and answering his questions. They would often end up at the restaurant together, and while Yui savoured her sea urchins and told them not to worry about her, Takeshi and Shio would open up heavy medical textbooks, full

139

of the teenager's Post-it notes and annotations, and talk.

Knowing that Shio had no parents, Takeshi felt a certain sense of responsibility towards him. He wanted to help him, but how? When Shio mentioned a scholarship to study in Tōkyō the following year, Takeshi thought he could finally do something concrete. He gathered information about all the possible universities the young man could apply for. *What do you think of this one? And how about this one?* He would pass him prospectuses that he had travelled all over the city to collect, and helped him compare them. And what about his speciality? Had he thought about it yet? This was an important decision that would completely determine the direction of his career. Also, what kind of doctor did he want to become? One who worked with patients or one who wrote articles to publish in journals? And another thing – could he speak English? That was an essential tool. You couldn't really do without it.

Shio never spoke about his family. Only about how much he was studying and the things he saw each day. At the hospital, in the street, in the canteen. He was enthusiastic about all of Takeshi's suggestions. He wanted to turn his life around, wanted to get out of there.

It wasn't until a year later that Yui and Takeshi learned the truth about Shio's father.

chapter

twenty-eight

*Three Examples of Discoveries from the
Pages of Shio's Mother's Books*

1. A *momiji* leaf at page 56 of Kamiya Mieko's book
   Ikigai Ni Tsuite [On *Ikigai*], Tōkyō: Misuzu Shobō,
   1966.
2. Two pine needles at page 20 of *Otogibanashi no
   wasuremono* [Lost Property Fairy Tales], text by
   Ogawa Yōko and illustrations by Higami Kumiko,
   Tōkyō: Shūeisha, 2006.

3. Two violets, one *higan-bana* flower and a cicada's wing at pages 5, 33 and 50, respectively, of the Ishida Tetsuya catalogue, *Tetsuya Ishida – Complete*, Tōkyō: Kyūryūdō, 2010.

Note: Shio's real name was Shiori. But one day his mother made him a hot chocolate and he put salt in it instead of sugar, and from then on he became known to everyone as 'Shio' 塩, salt.

chapter

twenty-nine

*S*HIO ALWAYS LIFTED THE RECEIVER and said 'Dad' first. Then he'd ask how he was, what he was up to and why he was still *over there*. He'd say his brother had been leaving the house less and less, his room was a pigsty and their aunts were suffocating him (they asked thoughtfully, but constantly, what they could do to make things better, but how was he supposed to know?). It was about time their dad came back. Shio couldn't handle it all by himself.

Otōsan, Father, Dad, he called him; he would beg using the same formula, the words feeling emptier each time he uttered them. Sometimes he would even insult him.

'He insults him? How do you know?'

'He told me,' Suzuki-san replied, the day Takeshi talked to him about the documents Shio would need for the scholarship.

'What scholarship?' he asked. 'Where?'

They had finally decided on Tōkyō Medical University, the one where Shio hoped to specialise. The scholarship would cover all of the enrolment costs, his tuition fees and the rent for a room in the university halls of residence.

'Really? Shio? In Tōkyō?' Suzuki-san was taken aback.

Yes, yes, Takeshi confirmed, and reiterated that he felt Shio had a real shot at getting the scholarship. His grades were good and, as sad as it was, his being an orphan would likely help his case.

'Shio isn't ready to move away from here,' Suzuki-san replied.

146

'But it's been three years,' Yui said slowly, wary of sounding judgemental.

'No, I'm not talking about his mother's death; he seems to be coming back from that. It's more his father. The man still needs him, and Shio won't be able to leave him anyway.'

Leave him? What did that mean? Takeshi became suspicious; there was something dark in Suzuki-san's words.

It happened rarely, but it did happen, Suzuki-san said. That people came to Bell Gardia not to talk to the dead, but to the living.

Yui and Takeshi looked at one another, in shock. They had heard him right: Shio's father wasn't dead. Suzuki-san had met him in person once when the boy had tried to bring him here, hoping it would help his father to find himself again.

On 11th March 2011 Shio's father's boat, to avoid running into the shore, set a course out to sea, hoping to ride out the tsunami. But the strength of the wave meant that the vessel was slung into that grotesque position in the middle of the city, teetering on the top of a building like a trophy. A few years on, it had become one of the most iconic images of the disaster.

There were those immense curling waves, and the boat had repeatedly climbed skywards to then plunge back down into the sea. Later that day, the man was told about the wild terror on his face. You see, he wasn't alone on the boat; there was a woman with him.

It wasn't the initial fury of the tsunami that had crushed Shio's father, but rather, as the hours passed, the terrible, incessant suction of the sea and the silence that pressed down over the bay. Among the debris drawn outwards, Shio's father saw dozens of bodies, cadavers skewered by wooden planks or twisted into distorted positions. Their eyes wide open, like soldiers fallen in battle.

The woman, curled up in the cabin, urged him to come away from the side of the boat, because there were some things that, once seen, could never be forgotten. But he'd retorted that people were dying out there, drowning like ants, and if there were any survivors, even just one, he needed to save them.

He had made a futile effort with a fishing rod and a net to grab a floating boy with an enormous wound on his head; the boy was wearing the uniform of his son's high school. He had pressed his hands into his eyes, wailing, when he'd seen a newborn baby and her mother in one of those half-floating boxes that were once cars, dozens, hundreds of them, traps in which scores of people drowned; like the little goldfish you could win at a fair, limp in their plastic bags before you had time to get them home.

As the hours passed, before Shio's father's eyes, humans were transformed into sea creatures: thin-limbed elderly folk became crabs, men dragged away by the current were carp, their hungry mouths agape. In an instant, houses and shops became rocks, life rafts to cling on to to avoid drowning.

But the worst thing of all was that he didn't save anyone, not even the man who was hurled against the side of his boat and who didn't give up climbing until his very last breath.

Shio's father felt a pang of familiarity when he saw him. He must have been fifty, and was soaked from top to bottom except the crown of his head, where a little dry patch signified his resistance.

'Come on!' he had shouted repeatedly. But the man never said a word. He didn't say anything, not when their fingers clasped for a moment, nor when Shio's father, terrified by the prospect of falling in himself, loosened his grip. And as the man was sucked up by the sea, disappearing behind the carcass of a house that was crumbling into the water, Shio's father remembered. The man was the owner of the bakery he used to go after work on a Saturday afternoon. The one who cheerily claimed that his *melon pan* was the best *melon pan* in all of Japan.

One rumour said that Shio's father had mistaken someone else's body for his wife's. Another that he really had seen her and was crushed by remorse.

The truth was that his powerlessness had destroyed him. The woman had been right: some things can never be unseen.

On that day he fell into a trance. He became kelp, just like the stuff he used to spend hours untangling and separating, hanging one end this side of the wooden plank and one the other, to be dried by the breeze. His body was intact but his mind was somewhere else.

So now Shio used the Wind Phone to talk to his father who was alive and living under the same roof, and not with his mother who had been recorded missing. He refused to call her, he said, because she still had to be out there somewhere. He secretly hoped that one sunny day she would come home to stick the two parts of his father back together again.

Sometimes he wondered if this was her revenge for her husband's betrayal. She had taken a piece of him away, the best piece.

'What an awful story,' Yui had murmured. 'There's no way to . . .'

She was about to say 'fix him', but she stopped herself.

Since moving to Tōkyō she had seen people wandering around like broken toys: they always stayed at the edges of the crowd, on the margins of the lives of millions of others who set their alarms at the same time, stood judiciously in line on the platform, got on and off the trains in unison, uttered *ohayō-gozaimasu* and *otsukaresama-deshita* dozens of times a day, swallowed their own saliva, inhaled the exhalations of others, flopped down, stood up at the last stop on the last train, and then started off once more.

She thought again of the man in the school gym with his picture frame. Her heart suddenly softened, even though she knew these were two very different stories.

Takeshi waited before replying to Suzuki-san.

'Wouldn't it be good for him, for precisely that reason, to get away for a bit?'

Takeshi had always believed in the power of distance.

'Sometimes you need a change of scenery,' he added, 'even if it's just to take stock of things.'

'They've tried, but Shio has refused every time. He says yes to begin with but, when it comes down to it, he doesn't go through with it. He's convinced that his father will wake up one day.'

'But is that possible?' Yui asked, looking at Takeshi.

'With the right treatment it's not impossible, but it would take a long, long time . . .'

That day in the car on the way back to Tōkyō, Yui and Takeshi hardly spoke.

Since they had started visiting Bell Gardia, they had begun to see humanity differently. The lives of many people had collided with theirs, within the walls of Suzuki-san's living room or outside, on the streets of Ōtsuchi and Kujira-yama. And sometimes these lives, like Shio's, became grafted onto their own.

Why hadn't the boy told them about his father? Why had he said he was dead?

It was probably because to him, in a way, his father was more dead than his mother was. And because, however insignificant it may sound, Shio was ashamed, not just of his father, but of himself for the way he had reacted to what had happened. He thought a clean-cut tragedy would be easier to explain, would help him keep up a good impression.

As they arrived in Tōkyō, Takeshi broke the silence. 'He'll tell us about it himself when he feels ready.'

'Yes, I'm sure he will,' Yui replied immediately.

There was less and less need, between them, to specify the subject of their conversation.

chapter

thirty

Shio's Favourite Passage from the Holy Bible

After forty days Noah opened a window he had made in the ark and sent out a raven, and it kept flying back and forth until the water had dried up from the earth. Then he sent out a dove to see if the water had receded from the surface of the ground. But the dove could find nowhere to perch because there was water over all the surface of the earth; so it returned to Noah in the ark. He reached out his hand and

155

took the dove and brought it back to himself in the ark. He waited seven more days and again sent out the dove from the ark. When the dove returned to him in the evening, there in its beak was a freshly plucked olive leaf! Then Noah knew that the water had receded from the earth. He waited seven more days and sent the dove out again, but this time it did not return to him.

Genesis 8:6–12

chapter

thirty-one

WHEN HER DAUGHTER WAS BORN, Yui had been amazed. Even the tiniest of lives needed everything: plates, cutlery, crying, a full refrigerator, lullabies and vaccinations. She got used to it quickly, though she didn't feel she was much good at the more practical side of things.

She diligently filled out the *boshi techō*, the little mother and child handbook that she'd been given at the city hall before her daughter was born. Every week during the pregnancy she had noted down her weight and blood pressure. After the birth she copied out the baby's measurements precisely: 2,739 grams, 47 centimetres long. Between the measurements she added: ten fingers and ten toes, a mountain of dark hair, cries like a lunatic.

Anyone who has experienced great grief wonders at some point which is more difficult, learning or unlearning. There was a time when Yui wouldn't have been able to say, but now she was sure it was the second.

After her daughter died, Yui took a ruler and marker pen and drew a diagonal line from the bottom left to the top right of every empty page. When her daughter was still alive, Yui had developed a sequence of physical actions so that even when her mind failed her, her body could help out. Sometimes, though, she still found herself counting the months until the next vaccination on her fingers, or writing down something she needed to buy for her, and that's when she understood that once the mind has learned something, it doesn't give it up easily.

★ ★ ★

Yui had her doubts about the umbilical cord. According to folklore, it could protect a child from any threat and could snatch life back from death, even in the depths of critical illness. It was supposed to be crushed into a fine powder and swallowed by the sick child.

The small box was given to her the day after the birth, still open so that the little piece of flesh wouldn't go mouldy as it dried.

Even though she was rather untidy by nature, Yui had looked after it with great care. Following the tradition, she would have given it to her daughter on her wedding day.

She dropped the little blackened piece, unable to crumble it up, into the urn that reunited her mother and daughter. She had taken the ashes and bones of both of them and gently tipped one into the other, keeping them together just as they had been found. Holding each other.

'Holding each other?' Takeshi asked one evening in the car as they were driving back to Tōkyō from Bell Gardia. He imagined a beautiful scene but was cautious not to ask too much.

159

Yui nodded. She had her hands on the wheel.

It had been a beautiful day. There had been a barbecue with lots of people from the local area. Around thirty people from Ōtsuchi had come, including seven children. The old woman with the dog had called in with some *azuki*-bean paste pancakes and told them that her German daughter-in-law was pregnant. Suzuki-san's wife had made some delicious *chirashi-zushi*. Keita, amid the general euphoria, announced that he had passed his university entrance exams: he would be going to the University of Tōkyō, Tōdai, following in his mother's footsteps.

Perhaps it was because of the joy she had felt that day, or because of their Bell Gardia anniversary, which coincidentally fell on the same day ('Do you know it's been two years since you both came here for the first time?' Suzuki-san had said, showing them the little book in which he recorded everyone who visited), that Yui felt strong enough to speak about it.

'Yes, they were holding each other.'

She told him that when the people at the

information centre had explained that they thought
her mother and her daughter had been found and,
depending on the state of the bodies, they would
need either an identification or a DNA test, she had
become terrified by the idea of seeing them. What
if, from then on, she could only remember them like
that?

However, it turned out that having seen them was
her only consolation, the confirmation of her hope,
that they didn't die alone, but together.

'They told me they had a photo to show me, as
long as I was willing to see it. It was up to me. So I
asked them to describe it to me first. They said they
had found them in an embrace, that they looked alive
and that, as tragic as it was, it was a remarkably tender
image. They were all moved when they saw it.'

They had found them locked together, like a closed
clamshell.

'It was incredible, I can't describe it, it looked as
though my mother's hands were tied around my
daughter's body. It seemed like they were sleeping.'

★ ★ ★

The volunteers who recovered them had placed a finger over their lifeless jugulars and beneath their smoke-filled nostrils following protocol, but they also had the fore-sight to imagine a third person (a son? a daughter?) that connected these two people. If that person was still alive, they thought, they would want to see this.

So they took a photo. And only after that did they untangle them.

'They were good people,' Takeshi murmured, looking out of the window. After a long stretch of mountains the ocean appeared again on the left. Tōkyō was close now. When Yui saw it, immense and black before her, she slowed the car down.

Again? she just had time to wonder, quickly reaching towards the chocolate. But this time the nausea was overwhelming.

'Pull over,' Takeshi said. He pointed towards a lay-by just up ahead. It was as though he had it in the palm of his hand, offering it to her.

Yui got out quickly, leaving the keys dangling in the ignition.

She stood with the sea head-on, looking it in the face.

Here it was, again. She was looking at the ocean and, in it, seeing everything.

The water advancing, the debris piled up at the sides of the roads like snow.

Her two by three metres canvas in the gymnasium. The man with the bulging eyes who observed her from the other side of his picture frame and clearly pronounced the caption he had created for her: 'The lady who doesn't eat. The lady who watches the sea instead of the TV.'

The bodies she had seen at the morgue, pieces of flesh to which they tried in vain to attach a name. The teeth they extracted to recover an identity.

And the sea, that immense sea that Yui went out to look at every day. Hugging the tree and at the same time holding on to the strongest thing in the world: the life that was still within her, in spite of herself.

The images were coming back up, one after another and then rolling again from the beginning. They pushed up in her chest, desperate to come out.

For the first time since her nausea had started, Yui did nothing to stop the surge, and out it came.

Retch after retch she felt as though she was being liberated of litres of salty water and debris from the disaster, of the foul sludge she had kept down for years out of fear that her memories would flow out with it. The joy, for instance, that she had felt the day her daughter was born, or the satisfaction of having managed to bring her up with more yeses than nos. Or the intense happiness of covering her in little kisses to wake her up every morning. Or, of her mother, the hand she always placed on Yui's back as she said *Itterasshai* when Yui left the house, or the phrase she had said so many times Yui was sick of it: 'Yui-*chan*, what a wonderful daughter you are.'

Takeshi rested a hand on her back, not saying anything. In the fist of his other hand he held Yui's ever-longer and blacker hair, the yellow strip still visible around the tips.

When there was nothing but air left inside her, Yui crouched down. She felt the need to hug herself tight.

She didn't cry, but neither did she take her eyes off the sea for a single moment. She understood now that there would be no more nausea ever again, even though she had come to accept it as something that would be with her for life.

She had been wrong. It isn't just the best things that come to an end, but also the worst.

Takeshi remained behind her, careful not to obstruct her view. He rubbed her back, first from the bottom to the top as she threw up, and then in the other direction, to help her breathe in the wind that was still blowing against them.

'I was lucky,' Yui whispered once she had recovered, knowing deep down that it was the truth. 'At least I got to see them one last time.'

There were people who had searched for bodies for years, who'd had to give up on the idea of ever finding them. And if you didn't see them one last time, the grief had no end.

Perhaps it was the intense darkness of that stretch of road, but before getting back in the car and continuing the journey to Tōkyō, Yui rested her gaze on the puddle of vomit that now trickled over the side of the mountain.

It was black, gleaming, like the devil in fairy tales.

'Black as tar.'

'I don't know what colour it was, Yui, but—'

'It was like a horror film, wasn't it? Go on, say it!'

'Seriously, I've never seen any patient vomit like that.'

They would laugh until they reached Tōkyō, they would laugh so much at the stupid description and her cartoonish retches that they would have to pull over again. To laugh even more, until they cried, clutching their stomachs.

They laughed so much they couldn't breathe.

chapter

thirty-two

The Tradition of heso no o へその緒, *as the Obstetrician Who Helped her Give Birth Explained it to Yui*

'This custom of giving the new mother the umbilical cord has been followed in Japan for centuries. The cord has been carrying nutrients from mother to baby for months. So, if you think about it, along with the placenta, it's the most precious thing there is.

'It is believed to be a sort of talisman that can

protect the unborn child throughout its life. Mothers used to give it their sons when they left for war and to their daughters when they got married.

'It is also said that, in the case of a fatal illness, we should grind it to a powder, add water and imbibe it, and it will save us. Wonderful, isn't it?

'Leave it there, open. Now it's white and shiny, but by tomorrow it will be all dry and brown, no bigger than a peanut.'

chapter

thirty-three

'YOU NEED PRACTICAL THINGS TO set you straight.'

This was the beginning of a long speech. Takeshi could tell from the way his mother's hands were suspended in mid-air.

'The telephone, you see, is a practical thing.'

Takeshi scraped the leftovers from dinner into one bowl, then stacked the empty crockery, sliding one small dish into another and gathering up the chopsticks.

'I saw a photograph of the Wind Phone. It's like the ones we used back in my day – in your day too actually, right? The middle part looks like a necklace, or a Buddhist rosary,' said the woman, miming a circle around her wrist. 'One of those bracelets monks wear, you know?'

How many similes does one word need, Takeshi thought.

He sighed. Dinner was finished. He got up from the table as his mother peeled a tangerine, its perfume dispersing along with its peel, and he rested the stack of dishes next to the sink.

His mother had never been a woman who kept men out of the kitchen. On the contrary, she had brought him up with the conviction that there was no difference between a son and a daughter.

As his mother continued to talk about the phone box, Takeshi muttered countless *sō desune, hontō da ne* – 'it's true, yes, yes, I agree, you're right' – and other sounds that didn't even make it as far as words. That usually calmed her down.

'You'll see; it'll help and she'll start to feel like going out and having fun again. A child has to play at her age, she absolutely has to play.' The weight of her phrase pressed down on the *has to*. 'If she doesn't play now, when will she?'

'I know,' Takeshi finally interrupted. 'But these things take time; the paediatrician said so too.'

Had the doctor really said that? He couldn't remember now. He might have done, but Takeshi was no longer sure. He knew, though, that the authority of a third party, preferably a man, was the only way to stop his mother.

'Some things take time, but some things will keep burrowing down if you leave them . . . and if you don't do something, the marks will remain. Try not to overdo it either though,' she replied.

It had now been more than two years since Hana last spoke; if his mother was talking about scars, they were already far beyond that point, and nobody was under any illusions. But Takeshi didn't said anything. He knew it was best to stay quiet when someone believed something so simple could fix everything.

'You'll see, she'll get better, I'm sure. Take her to Bell Gardia and show her how it all works.'

171

From the window the sky seemed to spill over Mt Fuji, the clouds strangling its slopes. The train ran along the base of the mountain, the pairs of tracks snaking closer together then venturing apart again. Takeshi had thought about moving house after his wife's death, but then he realised how much he loved the view from the window that changed every day.

'The first time you told me about the telephone, I thought of the *butsudan*. If you think about it, the *butsudan* also helps us to live with the idea that everything comes to an end. It's like always having a little bit of death in the house.'

Takeshi agreed. The household altar was a custom upheld in many Japanese homes. Some people chose not to have one, because of the maintenance it required, but it was undeniable that it helped people to become more familiar with death and the possibility of establishing a different relationship with our loved ones after they've gone.

'When I was a little girl, you know, it taught me that things are still there even when we can't see them anymore; that when people disappear from our everyday lives, it doesn't mean they vanish completely. Like my grandparents on my mother's side, who died long before I was born, or the two brothers I had who were dead by the time my mother gave birth to them. They were invisible, but that didn't mean they weren't there. They had just moved home, so to speak; from the kitchen or the bedroom into the living room, onto the *butsudan*. One day my grandparents were over here, the next they were there.'

Takeshi nodded, remembering the profile of his great-grandparents in the only photo he had ever seen of them. The picture was taken in the severe style of back then: the woman sitting, in a *kimono*, the man standing beside her. Their facial expressions were formal and haughty. Takeshi's mind wandered; when did we start smiling in photographs?

'And these are things that as a child you can only understand through the idea of magic, or a gentle religion like our one,' the woman continued. 'And I tell you, talking to my parents once they were dead was a lot easier than it was when they were alive. They would always hush me up, saying, "You're the youngest, so be quiet." It's rather funny when I think about it now, because I'd always be the youngest, wouldn't I?'

Takeshi picked up the tangerine peel that was left on the table, threw it into the bin and started pushing it down for the waste collection.

'The *butsudan* gives me that kind of consolation; I feel as if your father is still here with me.'

Takeshi remembered his mother being in constant dialogue with his father, who had passed away when she was forty and he, who had married her in his fiftieth year, was twenty years older. He mostly remembered her interminable outbursts and the figure of that fair, impassive man standing patiently and listening. She would pour the overflowing bucket of her day out onto the table and he would search through the sand, turning over every microscopic fragment of shell until she was happy.

And now, in front of the household altar where he too rested, the woman would kneel down with her back erect, light the incense, offer some sweets and rice and invoke him to listen to her again, just like she did when he was alive. Her son would often find her asleep in the *tatami* room, her upright pose turned horizontal, her head resting on the *zabuton*.

'Yes, you're right,' she happily responded when Takeshi reminded her of that. 'Your father loved me that way, chatty and chaotic.'

And her laughter swallowed up the tinge of sadness that overcame her whenever she felt too old or too stupid to make things better.

'On the subject of bringing Hana to Bell Gardia, I'm going to ask my friend what she thinks,' Takeshi returned to their previous conversation to wrap it up. 'It might be worth a try.'

'The friend you always go up to Iwate with?'

'Yes, I was thinking of her. Yui's more observant than I am. She'll know whether it's a good idea to take Hana there or not,' Takeshi said. 'Let's go to bed.'

He switched off the light on the cooker hood, which was illuminating one last square of the kitchen, and their shadows slipped away.

chapter

thirty-four

The Ten Most Vivid Memories Takeshi Had of his Father

When they went up the Tōkyō Tower for the first time and saw how huge the city was.

His habit of unscrewing and rescrewing the caps of bottles at the table.

The way he drummed his fingers on things.

The clumsy and confusing way he tried to explain how babies were made.

The times he would go into the other room and phone his younger sister. The intense conversations he had with her in a low voice.

The little model Ferrari he brought back from a trip to Italy.

When he saw him cry for the first and last time: his little sister had died.

When they went to see *rakugo* in Asakusa together.

The day he found him in his armchair, stock-still, with the newspaper at his feet. He looked like he was sleeping, but he'd had a heart attack.

His peaceful face as he lay in the coffin, the flowers (mostly lilies) scattered all around him, along with crossword puzzles and his favourite sweets (*manjù*).

chapter
thirty-five

TAKESHI REALISED EARLY ON THAT the most important thing Akiko, his wife, wanted to teach their daughter was trust.

Of course, like all mothers, she harboured the constant fear that something would happen to her child. A bad thing, mostly, and that this bad thing would happen at the hands of another person. 'I fear objects less and less,' she said. The solid materials of the world, cars for example, or tumbling down on a sloping pavement. It was Hana's childish attempts to

179

make eye contact with passers-by that worried her, such as the gaze of a slightly depraved-looking old man.

Yet when it came to choosing between fear and trust, Akiko always opted for the latter.

The only argument Takeshi could remember having had with his wife was when she and Hana had been walking home from the cafe one day after breakfast and Hana had walked up to a homeless man in the street to proudly show him her drawing. 'Look, look!' she had exclaimed, and Akiko, rather than pulling her daughter out of the man's reach, got Hana to sit down on the edge of the pavement and have a conversation with him.

It was necessary to instil a bit of suspicion in children, didn't she understand? It was up to the adults to teach them, Takeshi said later that evening, as soon as he was sure Hana was asleep. Children don't recognise danger, they don't even know what death is: if Hana saw the carcass of an insect, she would probably think it was sleeping. If an adult didn't hold her hand at the level crossing, she would probably run in front of a train with her arms wide open.

No! Akiko replied fiercely. Being afraid of life and of people only makes you weaker. It was up to them, she said, to protect Hana until she was capable of protecting herself. But first they needed to teach her joy.

'Knowing how to love life is a necessity, Takeshi, and she needs to learn to trust people. Not to hate them, there's no way out of hate,' she said, lowering her voice.

Then she immediately hugged her husband tight, the way she'd learned to do with their daughter whenever the little girl got carried away in a tempestuous tantrum for reasons Hana herself wasn't even sure of.

That night they would make love, thinking perhaps it was the right time to give Hana a brother or sister. Three months later, while searching for the signs of pregnancy, Akiko discovered the tumour.

Childhood disappears for everyone. All children die one day.

So Hana would disappear one day too, her father thought. He needed to help her find her childhood again, fast.

Giving up work because of the pregnancy had hit Hana's mother hard: she had been studying to become a singer since she was four years old and the complications of the pregnancy, which had kept her bed-bound for five months, had made singing difficult. The fact that nobody was forcing her to give it up, and that Takeshi and his mother were always offering to look after the baby once it was born, didn't make the decision any easier. She was sure she had to do it.

After Hana was born, she and Akiko lived in a state of absolute symbiosis, the mother appearing to need her baby even more than the baby needed her mother. Akiko's career was over and she didn't have the courage to go back to it after the break that she herself deemed too long. It undoubtedly weighed on her, yet her love for Hana was an immense thing and she often mentioned how much she enjoyed spending her days with her.

She could have asked for help from her mother-in-law, who lived nearby and wasn't working, but as a child she'd been told hundreds of times that 'Our choices shape our lives,' and she really wanted to see what kind of life would come out of the choices she had made. On top of that, she struggled with her mother-in-law's loquacity, and she didn't like the woman's habit of rolling up Takeshi's shirtsleeves, or of stroking his hand at the end of a meal. She found the way the old woman corrected Hana bewildering, and didn't understand why she had to ruffle the elaborate hairstyles Akiko did for her daughter in front of the mirror every morning. She was jealous, to the point where a sort of affectionate rivalry emerged between them.

The mother-in-law admired her daughter-in-law. She didn't always understand her – for example how Akiko could be so melancholic one day and so happy the next; and she couldn't fathom how such variation could exist within one person. And yet it was optimism that prevailed in the young wife, and that alone she found astonishing.

Takeshi's mother had spent twenty years clearing her name of the scoldings she had subjected her son to, especially during that long period of confusion after her husband passed away and she found herself left alone to manage a life that, practically speaking, she'd had little to do with until that point. She could forgive herself only by recalling the difficulties of her own childhood.

On second thoughts, it was a miracle that her son had got a degree (in medicine!), and that was something she told herself every time she worried she had thrown her life away: my son, the doctor! A son who saves people's lives!

Yet when she was with friends or strangers, she hid this amazement. Taking his success for granted made her look as though she was perfectly at home in this lifestyle, in the luxurious apartment in Naka-Meguro, the eternally fresh flowers in the hallway, her granddaughter's private kindergarten.

She also felt she'd accumulated a certain amount of credit from the struggles in her life. A good companion for her son and a nice daughter-in-law for herself was the least she deserved.

And there was Akiko, who swooped in like Mary Poppins to the house of the Banks family. What she loved most about that girl with the melodious voice was the way she was with Takeshi and their little girl. She was extremely precise when it came to looking after the house and she never forgot a birthday or to pay a bill. And yet she was also a dreamer, and she had the inborn lightness of someone who never stamps her feet when things don't go her way.

That's where Akiko's beauty came from: she knew how to let go. Unlike her, her daughter-in-law didn't make a big fuss when things went wrong. Sure, she ate a little too much (she was crazy about banana special eclairs and would never dream of sharing them), and she was always kissing Takeshi and their daughter. Also, she was definitely excessively sentimental, as women sometimes are when they sacrifice themselves for their family, but the joy and the trust she embodied were rare. However hard she tried, Takeshi's mother would never have that level of courage.

But then Akiko got sick and, as if a rift had opened up in the earth, everything collapsed.

★ ★ ★

185

Two weeks after the funeral, when they realised that the little girl's silence was more than a passing phase, Takeshi's mother feared that it was a direct consequence of her mother's love. *If we are destined to lose certain things, wouldn't it be better to do without them from the start?* she wondered, not sure of the answer.

At first, putting on a brave face, she told herself that at least she was still around, a young grandmother in good health.

Takeshi didn't do enough; he handled Hana like a precious china doll. But really, she was no better. As the months went on, she developed a distant fear of this soundless creature whose innermost thoughts she couldn't begin to imagine.

Would Hana always bear the marks of having lost a mother who was so special?

The old lady would poke her head round the door of Hana's little bedroom and ask if she wanted to go out for a walk or watch the TV together, but the girl would shake her head and go back to cutting and folding *origami* or flicking through picture books by herself. The thing she most loved was standing at

186

the window and watching the trains go by, passing through the neighbourhood and then vanishing again.

Hana wasn't ready to let anybody take her mother's place.

Takeshi's mother just hoped there had been enough time for Akiko to instil in her daughter that remarkable sense of joy, untouched by whatever else was going on in the world.

As the months went by, she found comfort in her son's frequent mentions of this new person, Yui. All she knew of this woman were the digits of her phone number and her profile picture of a ballerina dressed in red, flying through the air. Not that there was anything going on between them, not that she knew of. But who knows, she would think when she needed a dose of hope, perhaps she'll be the bandage that heals this beautiful, bruised family.

She started to include Yui's name in her daily prayers before the *butsudan*.

chapter

thirty-six

*Ten Things Plus One that Hana and Akiko
Loved Doing Together*

1. Counting the *kan kan*s at the level crossing and
    losing count when the train passed.

2. Pressing all the odd-numbered buttons in the lift.

3. Saying *'Akkanbe! Bero bero be!'* and sticking their
    tongues out.

4. Going to the Mori Building to see Tōkyō from above, asking each other 'Where's our house?' and pointing at random.

5. Playing trains (Hana would grab onto the strap that Akiko had connected to her handbag, and Akiko would say, *Choo, choo. Off we go!*).

6. In cherry-blossom season, running back and forth along the bank of the river in Naka-Meguro, at dawn, before the crowds arrived. Then pretending to speak an invented language when surrounded by tourists.

7. Saying 'I'm as full as an elephant!'

8. Taking the Inokashira line and getting off at Eifuku-chō to eat a pizza.

9. Opening their mouths when it rained and saying, 'How delicious! Compliments to the chef!'

10. Greeting all the *tanuki* statues next to restaurants and private houses.

11. Ordering three slices of cake at the cafe, all different flavours, and then cutting them into five pieces and playing *jan ken* for the fifth piece.

chapter

thirty-seven

'WHAT DO YOU THINK? SHOULD we try bringing Hana to Bell Gardia?' Takeshi asked her that evening in a text message.

Yui said she didn't know. But her first thought was that perhaps it would be best to explain to Hana how the Wind Phone worked, tell her about the journey, the garden, how it made her dad feel. Make a story out of it. And then, if she seemed curious, invite her to join them the following Sunday. But not to put any pressure on her.

Takeshi followed her advice.

In the evening, after the usual goodnight story, he read his daughter a children's picture book about the Wind Phone.

He told her that this was how he talked to her mother and kept her up to date with how he and Hana were doing. He felt close to her there and felt sure that she was listening.

The journey? Well, the journey was very, very long, but they saw the most wonderful views.

'The sea, Hana – do you know how many colours there are in the sea in winter?'

That same night, Yui remembered a Friday five years earlier.

Her daughter was nearly two and they were on the train; she was screaming and Yui was trying, unsuccessfully, to calm her down. Now, looking back, she couldn't say whether they were howls of joy or distress, whether she wanted something Yui wasn't giving her (a biscuit? her phone?), or whether she was excited and expressing that in the only way she knew. Whichever it was, her voice was high-pitched and loud; it pressed against the walls of the carriage, and there was no sign she was going to let up soon.

Then somebody shouted, '*Urusai!*' Shut up!

Yui turned around in the carriage and saw a man with a heavy stomach, a white mop of hair and large thin-framed glasses that encircled his eyes. Eyes that were neither good nor bad. Just eyes.

Even before turning, Yui had instinctively said *sumimasen*. She was so used to apologising before doing anything else. When you had children you had to learn quickly to bow your head and seek forgiveness. It was just a few words, at the end of the day.

The thing that had been astonishing though, and that was coming back to her now, was the reaction of everybody else, including Hana. A silence had trickled over the carriage like honey, and everybody held their breath. And then, from the back of the train, from the mouth of a person of whom she could see only a small section of white hair, a song emerged.

Zō-san zō-san . . . Little elephant, little elephant, with a long, long nose.

And, as the song progressed, the voice cracked slightly in laughter. The most astonishing thing was that after the second verse, another voice joined in, then another. Yui was moved, and the elephant emerged, vivid in her mind, with its trunk, its heavy feet and the rest of its clay-like body.

Now the entire carriage seemed to be singing. It was as though she and her daughter had been parachuted into the middle of a wonderful party.

The man who had tried to mute her daughter had himself fallen silent. In his attempt to turn off one switch, he had inadvertently flipped another.

And now, switching off her bedside lamp, Yui smiled and thought that her daughter had a truly phenomenal power. Actually, she thought all children – without exception – were miracle workers.

chapter
thirty-eight

The Title of the Picture Book Takeshi Read to Hana that Evening

Yōko Imoto, *Kaze no denwa*, Tōkyō: Kinnohoshi, 2014.

chapter
thirty-nine

'**B**Y YOURSELF?'

As she nodded, her chin brushed the collar of her coat. Yes, she was sure.

'But by yourself? Are you really sure?'

The question played on a loop, continuously broadcast by both her father's voice and his expressive eyebrows. They furrowed one moment then stretched out again, unsure of how to respond.

'Come on. I'll walk you to the door and perhaps pick the phone up for you.'

Hana was inflexible. She crouched down, releasing herself from her father's grip.

He also squatted, bending his knees, and felt a twinge in his back. *What if I get old?* he asked himself. I can't get old. Not for another twenty years at least.

He raised his eyes and at the edge of the garden he saw Yui giving Suzuki-san the usual yellow package of banana cakes. She was talking to the man, bowing her head and smiling at him, yet Takeshi was certain that her attention was on him.

In that moment he wanted nothing more than for Yui to come home with them, for her to help him bring the shopping bags into the kitchen, to tidy up the little girl's wardrobe, for them to put up the New Year decorations together. It would be nice if they went to the temple together and prayed to the gods for a year of health and serenity. He wanted to keep her close, even when they became old and started to lose their hearing.

Oh dear, were they at that point? Could his feelings have grown that much already?

He wondered, bemused, whether Hana had noticed it too; children were so observant.

200

And would he ever be able to distinguish between the personal love he felt for a woman, and the plural love that encompassed his daughter?

Yui turned, pulled by the insistence of Takeshi's gaze, which, embarrassed, he immediately averted. He slowly stroked Hana's tangled hair.

'OK then, let's do it this way,' he said to his daughter. She would go in alone and he would wait outside.

The little girl detached herself from her father and approached the phone box with small steps, the bell in the archway jingling. Takeshi held his breath. What would happen? His racing pulse made him feel like a teenager.

Takeshi joined Yui just as Suzuki-san was going back into the house and Hana had picked up the telephone. They watched as the receiver moved down from the cradle to the little girl's ear.

'She's so small.'

'Not for her age,' Yui replied sweetly. 'She looks perfectly average to me.'

'I meant inside there.'

They stood unmoving on the doorstep.

He broke the silence. 'She wanted to go in alone.'

'Yes, I saw.'

'You don't need a voice to speak here, do you?' Takeshi asked.

'No, I suppose you don't.'

Takeshi shifted his position and inside the cabin he saw his daughter moving her mouth, her lips opening and closing over and over again.

He was stunned, unable to grasp a clearer emotion. Were her lips just beating the air or were they saying something? Was she speaking? Was Hana speaking?

'She's speaking!' he exclaimed. And then: 'Is she speaking?'

'It looks like she's speaking, yes,' Yui whispered.

'It's hard to say though.'

'No, we can't say with any certainty.'

'No?'

'It's difficult to tell from here. We're too far away.'

'But is she speaking?' Takeshi repeated.

'It does look like it.'

The wind blew vigorously, a pile of leaves swirling; a window slammed somewhere nearby, a dog barked.

The sounds were like a mist rising to veil the girl's privacy.

Yui, though she hid it, was just as excited as Takeshi was. She would have liked to hug him, but she didn't.

She stared at Hana's outline, which occupied little more than half of the glass squares her father's did. Another ten years or so and she'd catch him up.

chapter

forty

Phrases Floating on the Wind of Bell
Gardia in the Month of June

'I didn't love you then as much as I love you
   now.'

'It's always raining, I'm starting to get tired of it.'

'Auntie, where are you?'

'Hello, Grandpa? How do you pass the time where you are?'

'Seventy-two people died in a skyscraper in London.'

'If you come back, I swear, I swear . . .'

'Is it you who's hiding my things by any chance? I can't seem to find anything recently.'

'I found your diary; will you let me read it?'

'Mummy, it's Hana. Do you still remember me?'

'Dad?'

chapter

forty-one

W HEN NOBODY IS THERE TO see the miracle, the miracle happens.

Yui had met Hana for the first time that morning. After more than two years of listening to Takeshi talk about her, she was now looking into her eyes, holding her hand. Hana was docile and calm, the perfect example of a five-year-old girl. She would start elementary school the following year.

When Yui, rather than beeping the horn, had pulled over and got out of the car to meet them,

Hana smiled at her with a small bow. She seemed to know exactly who she was and why the three of them were all there together.

Yui had driven with extra care, casting frequent glances in the rear-view mirror to check that Hana, sitting in the child seat they had rented especially for the journey, was comfortable.

They had put the seat behind the driver, and Takeshi rode next to her.

They made their usual stop at the Lawson in Chiba. Hana chose a gianduja pudding and a little bottle of cocoa milk. She was crazy about chocolate and when the ocean came into view, Yui reached behind to offer her a square from her bar. Although she no longer felt so much as a spasm, she continued to buy it every time, she had got so used to the ritual.

'I see the sea and start salivating, but only because I've become greedy,' she said, amused. 'It's a disaster.'

She wanted chocolate regardless. She adored it.

'If I lived near the sea, I'd weigh a hundred kilos.'

Hana was comfortable around Yui straight away, as if she'd always been there. It was clear she liked her.

And when the little girl came out of the phone

box and ran towards her father's knees, hugging them tight, when tears came to both of their eyes and Yui made to leave them alone, it was Hana who grabbed the hem of her jacket, then her sleeve and finally grasped her hand, pulling her towards them.

It was the right moment. It always is when something beautiful happens.

Takeshi had to be ready for it, even before his daughter. He finally was. And Hana seemed to know.

And so, when Takeshi bent down to hug his little girl and she pushed her head into his neck, she began to speak again, and she said only normal things. Childish things, things that were just right for a girl her age.

She was hungry, and a bit thirsty too. No, the wind didn't bother her, even though it was very strong. It was really pretty there.

And although Hana would never be a chatterbox, she talked on the way home about how much she liked chocolate, and the two of them, she and Yui, bought a ton of sweets at a *konbini* they stopped at.

209

Takeshi watched them, amused, as they unwrapped, sucked, chewed, cracked, crunched and licked every single product that had the word *choco* on the packet.

Yui told her that when she was little, her mother would sometimes buy her two doughnuts. One for now and one for later. As if she really didn't want to teach her that happiness always came to an end.

'"You've finished one, but there's another one, you see," she would say. And the space in my stomach for the second one would quickly close up and that poor doughnut would be left to get old in the cupboard, nobody touching it.'

They could afford that luxury.

'Either way, there would always be another one.'

Hana's mouth opened wide in admiration.

'Your mummy also used to buy lots of sweets,' Takeshi cut in. 'More than she ever managed to eat.'

'Perhaps that's where your passion for chocolate comes from,' Yui said.

As if the two memories were connected in some way, Yui recalled a day in April, when her daughter's mouth was full, her cheeks bulging, and she said her first full sentence: *I want lots of cake*. It was Yui's

birthday and the little girl had come to help blow
out the candles. She remembered the feeling of her
warm and boisterous body on her lap. Her greedy
finger dipped into the cream, destroying its perfect
outline, and she brought it to her mouth.

'What's left in there?' Yui asked, nodding towards the
konbini bag. She decided to keep the memory of her
daughter to herself.

'Again? How much do you two eat?' Takeshi
would repeat over and over that evening, pretending
to be full, but only so that he could watch Yui and
Hana put something into their mouths and hear
them say: 'Mmmm! So good! Don't you think this
one's the best one? So crunchy, isn't it? It'd be delicious heated up a little in the microwave. With
cream on top! Yes, fresh cream on top! And
cinnamon powder! And cocoa? Yes, you're right,
cocoa powder too!'

Takeshi found Yui's ability to keep coming up with
new ways to describe the food entertaining, like those
TV presenters who invented other-worldly analogies
for something like a cream puff. He was moved by

211

his daughter's crystalline voice: it rested on things, on normal words, and made them vibrate with an exceptional timbre. Like fingertips on the keys of a piano.

chapter
forty-two

List of Chocolate Snacks Yui and Hana
Bought at the Konbini *on the Way Back*
from Bell Gardia

Gianduja and pistachio-cream doughnut

Chocolate-and-banana folded crêpe

Chocolate-filled *mochi*

Mini chocolate eggs with a whole almond inside

Chocolate sticks studded with crushed almonds and
hazelnuts

Chocolate-and-matcha cream-sponge sandwich

Soft sandwich filled with squares of chocolate

Small bag of 75% cocoa chocolates

Box of salted-caramel chocolate cubes

Chewy chocolate cookie

Packet of two crunchy biscuits with chocolate
chips

Can of cocoa milk x2

chapter

forty-three

THEY WOULD CONTINUE GOING TO Bell Gardia together. Not every month, because seven hours each way was really too much to ask of a child Hana's age, but the three of them would meet on a Saturday or Sunday, or Saturday *and* Sunday, in Tōkyō, to see a film at the cinema, eat pancakes shaped like flowers, or throw themselves repeatedly – sometimes up to fifty times in a row – down the slide of a park in the suburbs.

Of all the things they did together, one memory

echoed for longer in their minds. It was *O-bon*, a festival that fell in August, during Hana and Yui's summer holidays. It was to celebrate the return of people's ancestors, to welcome the dead back into their homes.

'Let's do things properly this year,' Takeshi announced.

They hung *chōchin* lanterns outside the front door, as custom dictated, so that the spirits could find their way home quickly without getting lost. Hana worked tirelessly making horses and oxen out of aubergines, cucumbers and toothpicks ('the horses are for a quick arrival, and the cows are for a slow return to the world of the dead'); Yui dug out her mother's recipe book and kneaded *mochi* and red bean paste to make *o-hagi*, and Takeshi went out and bought the flowers and offerings for the family altars, both theirs and Yui's.

Hana imagined her mother and paternal grand-father, whom she'd never met, riding on the saddle of the green bumpy horse, and alongside them, with the same lively gait, Yui's mother and daughter. The procession was so vivid in her mind that she drew it and gave her drawing to Yui, who took it home and taped it to the kitchen door. It cheered her up each time she walked into the kitchen.

On the evening of 16th August, Hana and Yui each put on a brightly coloured *yukata* and headed to the coast. Takeshi met them at the end of his shift at the hospital, he too wearing a *yukata* he had borrowed from a colleague, the *geta* sandals in his rucksack. He got changed quickly in the station toilets and the three of them set off, hand in hand, towards the strip of land that connected the little island of Enoshima to the mainland of Kanagawa.

Hana learned that, in the past, people believed that the afterlife was on the other side of seas and rivers, and so, in many places in Japan, people put offerings or candles on little paper boats, like lanterns, that they entrusted to the currents.

The two adults and the little girl bent down over their own paper boat, on which they had written the names of Takeshi's wife and Yui's mother and daughter. Spellbound, they watched the light of the candle flickering behind the inky *kanji*. Then, in unison, they opened up their hands and sent it off on the water, towards the open sea.

217

'This was a wonderful idea of yours,' Takeshi whispered, giving Yui's fingers a squeeze.

They continued walking towards the island and went up to pray at the shrine at the top of the mountain. Yui asked the goddess Benten for the ability to prepare delicious *bentō* for Hana's lunches, as she had never been a very good cook; Takeshi asked for more days like this one, and Hana just stared, enraptured, at the quivering reflections of the lanterns below. From up here they looked like fireflies flitting above the water's surface.

That night, Yui stayed at their house for the first time. She lay down beside Hana.

'Stay until I'm asleep,' the little girl pleaded.

'Is there something on your mind?'

'No, no, nothing,' she replied. She just wanted her there, in the same way a person might want a second coffee in the morning or an extra blanket in winter.

Yui nodded off too and Takeshi let her sleep. She would wake up with a terribly stiff neck and two deep furrows on her left cheek, but it would be worth it: the memory of their breakfast together would come back to her, like a gentle caress, for months to come.

When, some days later, Yui found a picture book that depicted, in pastel colours, all of the world's many heavens and celestial kingdoms, she bought it. She gave it to Hana when they were eating *sukiyaki* together at the end of a long day.

The origin of the world, according to Nigerian folklore, was a bull. According to the Altay Tatars, there were three fish that caused periodic floods to punish humans for their evil actions. In Sumatra, Indonesia, a serpent-dragon ruled the earth and the seven layers of heaven stacked above it, at the top of which there was a tree whose leaves bore everybody's destiny. They believed that earthquakes were caused by the movements of the serpent-dragon.

'Like in Japan!' Hana cried.

'Yes, just like in Japan,' Yui echoed, thinking of the *Ukiyo-e* prints that depicted the Japanese archipelago at the mercy of a catfish, the *namazu*, which caused disasters by whipping its tail and twitching its long whiskers.

They laughed as they read the book together; humans really are inventive.

Takeshi, who joined them after an exhausting shift at the hospital, particularly liked the world of the Yekuana people in Venezuela. On the sofa, with a glass of beer in front of him and a little bowl of salted *edamame* in his lap, he asked Hana and Yui whether they thought it could be possible that the Yekuana people were right, that the cosmos was modelled on a traditional house. After all, if a house was structured a certain way, why wouldn't the universe be the same?

But the idea they found most interesting was that of the Ojibwa tribe in Manitoba, Canada. For them, dreams were at the centre of everything. Dreams were what taught people about relationships between humans and non-humans and were how they explored unknown places, without the burden of the body.

'If you dream well, you'll have a long and beautiful life,' a grandfather in the book said to his grandson, and it reminded Yui of one of the first conversations she and Takeshi had ever had.

'Me reconceiving my daughter every night and you dishing out advice to Hana, do you remember?'

'Of course. We must have sounded like a right pair of nutcases.'

'But you were in fact her guardian spirit, without even knowing it,' Yui laughed later, when they were saying goodbye on the doorstep.

They would look through that book again every so often, and each time they came back to the story of the Ojibwa people. Hana preferred it over all the others, not just because of the dreams, but because they believed that dead people ended up in a spirit world where they didn't need to hunt for food and where, most importantly, there was no winter. Her mother used to get cold easily and Hana distinctly remembered her constantly complaining about how freezing the house was, how horrible it was to feel cold, that she even preferred the uncomfortably humid Tōkyō summers, despising the cold with every inch of her being (although she would then make the exact same protest against the heat in the summer). Hana liked the idea of a place where her mother wouldn't have to go around in woollen knee-high socks with a heat pack stuck to her stomach.

It was only once she had gone through the gate and was out on the street that Yui remembered she and her mother and daughter also used to share their dreams.

How had she forgotten that?

Yui, though she had never been a big talker, loved waking up in the morning and recounting what she'd dreamed about. When she was a child she used to tell her mother, and when she was an adult, her daughter. She tended to hold on to her dreams as if they had a deeper meaning, even if they didn't.

As she stirred the miso soup, she would describe what had happened during the night: who she had talked to, what they had spoken about, the places she had visited, who (if she could admit it) she had fallen in love with. And she did so as if it were an integral part of the morning routine, like preparing the rice or cutting the bread, as if it were inseparable from breakfast. And so her daughter, who would allow herself to be lulled by the cheery tones of her mother's voice, was quite used to fish or yogurt seasoned with Yui's nocturnal reveries.

On the train home, Yui stood by the door, despite the fact that the carriage was almost empty, and looked out at the silhouette of Tōkyō against the molten lava of the setting sun. She remembered the day her daughter had started to give back the gift of words. And what marvellous dreams she came up with. With instinct and emotion, she would randomly assemble various parts of her little life: explosions of dresses and flowers in fields of elephants and lions and dinosaurs, alongside her fears and prohibitions, the latter echoes of the words she heard over and over again during the daytime.

Yui remembered how this was the start of a new daily ritual of sharing their dreams, and whenever her mother came to see them early she loved to take part in the game too. If someone had walked into their kitchen on one of those mornings, they would have concluded that happiness runs in families.

As Yui opened the door onto the dense silence of her house, she concluded that memories were like objects, like the football that was found on the coast of Alaska a year after the tsunami, 3,000 miles away, on the other side of the Pacific Ocean.

Sooner or later, they always floated back to the surface.

chapter
forty-four

The Original Title of the Picture Book on the Afterlife that Yui Gave to Hana

Guillaume Duprat, *L'Autre monde. Une histoire illustrée de l'au-delà*, Paris: Le Seuil, 2016.

chapter

forty-five

$\mathcal{S}$PENDING TIME WITH HANA WAS the biggest test for Yui. Projecting her own daughter, the life she could have had, onto Takeshi's child was an involuntary but persistent instinct. It took time to put distance between the two girls, and to not feel guilty each time those thoughts came into her head. Imagining how Hana, in her own way, likely had the same concerns alleviated the anxiety that sometimes overwhelmed her.

However, just before they were due to meet one day, long into their relationship, a stray thought crushed Yui's mood. She imagined touching Hana, or giving her a kiss on the forehead, and not feeling anything. Absolutely nothing. Nice, sweet, but that was all, like any little girl, no different from a stranger she passed in the street.

Oh God, she wondered, *what if I'm really not ready to love her?*

I'll feel nothing, she threatened, *and I'll come out of it destroyed.*

But then she remembered a line, or even half a line, she had read in a book on raising children. She recalled it very clearly because it had unsettled her. It said that distance makes us love better and with greater respect. That distance wasn't, in fact, a bad thing. On the contrary, it was the lack of distance that could be harmful, and only the purest emotion, spontaneous and visceral love, was capable of healing a wound.

Ah, so, she remembered thinking, *love is dangerous.* And yet it's essential.

On the day of Hana's birthday, Takeshi organised a little dinner. In the afternoon they visited the shrine on the way back from the supermarket. Hana had chosen the evening's menu: fried oysters, potato salad, cream of corn soup and a cake with Kiki the Witch and her cat Jiji on it.

Yui, who was more observant than Takeshi, noticed that Hana was more interested in the animal than in the witch, and gave Takeshi a hint about the little girl's secret wish. Granting it was, ultimately, down to him.

It was November, and the temple was swarming with children dressed in *kimonos* in the bright colours of the *Shichi-go-san*, a festival for girls turning three and seven, and boys turning five.

'Are you sad that you didn't get to celebrate the festival for your third birthday?' Takeshi asked his daughter as the two of them climbed up the stone steps. An old woman carrying bags bumped into them but she was so wrapped up in her own grandson that she didn't notice.

'No, but I want to do it when I'm seven,' Hana quickly replied. She didn't like talking about the past and how much she'd missed.

Her father hurried to change the subject. 'Shall we buy an *ema* and hang it up?'

There was no need to ring the shop's bell. There were so many people coming and going that, despite the icy wind, the *miko* kept the sliding door open. Takeshi asked for the wooden plaque. On one side there was a print of three children dressed up in festival clothes in front of a *torii* gate, surrounded by maple leaves. Hana handed over the golden coin she had just been given by her father, then they moved to one side.

'So? What shall we write?' Takeshi asked, smiling. 'It's your day, your wish, you have to decide.'

'For our family to always be happy and healthy,' Hana replied, as if repeating a set phrase. Takeshi didn't question it. He put the bags down on the counter and took the lid off the pen given to them by the *miko*. He started to write the *kanji* that Hana would learn at school the following year.

'Which one says *family*?' she asked, examining the plaque.

Takeshi pointed at the two *kanji* for 'house' and 'tribe', and Hana placed the pad of her finger on 家族 – *kazoku*.

'Family?' she asked again, as if waiting for a definition. 'Daddy, Mummy, Grandma and Hana?'

'Yes,' Takeshi replied distractedly, rearranging the bags that were threatening to fall down.

'And Yui-san?'

Caught off guard, Takeshi hesitated.

An overexcited boy in blue ran behind them in the space before the altar while his relatives, no less excited than him, immortalised his breakaway through bulging hydrangea bushes and high stone lanterns on their smart phones.

'Do you think that when Yui-san thinks about her family, she thinks of us too?' asked Hana.

'I don't know . . .' Takeshi responded. 'But it would be nice if she did, wouldn't it?'

Takeshi watched as Hana nodded, but then her face darkened. It reminded him of her perennially sullen expression just after she was born, when his wife would pass her to him to hold and baby Hana would seem to scrutinise him, deciding whether to accept being held in his arms or burst into tears.

'What's up? Doesn't this make you happy?'

Hana stayed silent, staring at the ideograms penned along the veins of the wood. With her fingertip she started to tap the plaque along the lines that fell from

231

top to bottom, the two short sentences written from right to left, ending with her name.

'Her daughter was so pretty though,' she said.

'You mean Yui-san's daughter?'

Hana had seen photos of the little girl at Yui's house: licking an enormous ice cream that was about to fall, on a swing in her grandmother's arms, with her mouth wide open crying, with her eyes closed and sleeping. The shots were concentrated in a single frame above Yui's bed.

'Hana, do you mean Yui's daughter?' Takeshi repeated.

Her chin pressed against her collar, she cast her eyes downwards to avoid her father's gaze.

'But you're beautiful too!'

And she was; Takeshi had always thought it. And he was sure he was being objective in his judgement. Hana had sharp and intelligent eyes, and a long face like her mother's that resembled certain *Ukiyo-e* prints. She had slender hands, perfect skin, her expression was engaged and always present. Yes, beautiful. How else could he describe her?

The little boy who had been running around was

now screaming, held still by his mother who was struggling to tie up his loose *obi*. They could also hear the repetitive commands of someone further away, a photographer trying, with little success, to make a rigid and tense family smile under the reddest maple tree in the shrine.

Takeshi made an effort to focus on his daughter's emotions. She probably felt inadequate. Just like he sometimes did.

'Also, I'm really untidy,' Hana added, defeat in her voice now.

'Affection has nothing to do with how beautiful or tidy we are,' Takeshi said. His voice rose in his urgency to reassure her.

Hana went quiet, her gaze lost in the raucous vacuum of all those families. The *Shichi-go-san* celebration, the prayer to the gods to watch over the children, was noisy. According to Shintoism, until a child is seven, their fate is in the hands of the gods.

Takeshi knelt down so he could look into his daughter's eyes.

'Hana, love has nothing to do with beauty or talent, believe me.'

The little girl remained silent, fiddling with the edges of the *ema*. Then, in a faint voice, she asked, 'Really nothing?'

'Nope, nothing. Otherwise it would be a rather fragile thing, don't you think?'

Hana said nothing else, but she let her father stroke her head, which he took to be her agreement. Then, as if it to free herself from a conversation that was starting to get boring, she picked up the plaque and looked around for the iron bars to tie it to.

As soon as she'd seen them, she grabbed the *ema* and launched herself in the direction of the shrine, where families were still swelling and shrinking like swallows at dusk.

'Here?' she called, pointing at the dozens of other plaques hanging under the little wooden roof.

Takeshi smiled. 'Yes, tie it on there.'

She was too far away for his voice to reach her, so he gave an obvious nod and made an OK sign with his fingers.

Then he picked up the shopping bags and went to join her.

★ ★ ★

That evening, after Hana had blown out her six candles and devoured almost half of the cake, Yui, putting her to bed, explained why she'd chosen her present. It was a white wooden frame, with leaves tumbling down the sides.

She told her about the frame man at the shelter, blotting out the darker tones of the story. Then she explained that the whole world was cut up into frames: big windows, small windows, keyholes, the space between lines.

'And I think it's easier to understand the world when we look at it through them.'

Hana, already lying in bed, lifted the frame to her face and carefully observed her bedroom ceiling, where there were hundreds of stars twinkling from the projector her father had given her earlier that evening. Then she brought it down to examine Yui's face.

'Even the most enormous things can be cut up into tiny parts,' Yui whispered, stroking the little girl's cheek with her palm. 'Even the biggest problems. You can fit anything into a frame.'

chapter

forty-six

*The Definition of Family that Takeshi
Found that Evening in the Kōjien Japanese
Dictionary (Fifth Edition)*

かぞく【家族】
夫婦の配偶関係や親子-兄弟などの血縁関係によって
結ばれた親族関係を基礎にして成立つ小集団。社会構
成の基本単位。
　　➔ 家

Family

A small group that is established based on marital, parental or sibling relations. Basic unit of social composition.

→ House

chapter

forty-seven

Yui and Takeshi took things – everything – very slowly. They both knew that children understood little about life and that change had to be administered slowly. You could never predict how they would react to new things.

One Sunday morning the following January, they bought Hana a cage and made an appointment at the animal shelter.

The little girl had been restless for weeks: the thing she had not been able to give a name to on the day of her birthday had been getting bigger. It felt as if their bizarre family had grown out of a single magical bean planted by chance in their garden.

Hana wanted to wear her frilly dress and Kiki the Witch backpack. She asked her grandmother to stay in so that someone would be there when they got home.

The three of them – Hana, Takeshi and Yui – went together. Sitting on the spartan benches at the animal shelter, they listened patiently to the long and detailed lecture that was obligatory before adopting an animal. Yui took meticulous notes, accurately transcribing the statistics concerning the most common diseases in felines, sterilisation and the daily routines that should be respected for a successful cohabitation. She didn't want to miss anything.

Hana tried hard to understand all the sections, but she got lost in the diagrams, the percentages and the unfamiliar terminology that the vet used. Her father squeezed her shoulder when he saw her looking confused and she returned to staring at the bright screen and the vet's white shirt. Screwing up her face, she exerted all the effort and attention she could muster.

After the lecture they were taken into another room, where three kittens were curled up in a box. All different ages and colours, they each had a complicated backstory. Hana, overwhelmed by the idea of leaving two of them behind, asked her father for help choosing.

The decision was swift: they would take the little cat with black fur and lemon-yellow eyes called *Tora*, tiger, although she didn't look much like a tiger at all. She was thin and bony and put up very little resistance as she was lifted into the cage.

Of course it was important for Hana to learn how to look after something, her grandmother had whispered to Yui and Takeshi when she saw the cat for the first time, and having a pet was a good lesson in sharing space. But wasn't this one a bit scrawny? What if she died? Weren't they putting Hana at risk of yet another trauma?

But Takeshi was confident: the vet had said she was a very capable kitten who had survived as a stray.

She was stubborn, and that stubbornness meant she wouldn't die without putting up a fight.

It was true, though, that none of them had any experience with cats. Only Yui had owned a pet as a child, a mustard-yellow Welsh corgi with no tail that her mother had been given by a neighbour who was moving to Europe. Yui had fallen in love with that dog, making him the centre of her life. When he got sick, she felt like she was going to die too.

But she knew nothing about cats; in fact, from what she had heard, people who liked dogs couldn't like cats and vice versa. Worse than football fans. And so, as she always did when faced with something new, she bought many books on the subject and began to study. She read them on the metro on her way to work and in the advert breaks on the radio. Her colleagues teased her, saying *nyan nyan*, amused by the ever-growing mountain of books on her desk.

'And it's not even my own cat. Can you imagine!' she scoffed at herself.

★ ★ ★

At the till in the bookshop when they asked her if she wanted a paper book cover, Yui usually said no, she didn't need one. Who cared if people knew the title of the book she was reading? They were more than welcome to ruminate over her banal interests; Yui was not concerned about privacy in that sense.

But when she bought a manual on preparing children for elementary school and helping them get the most out of the school experience, she anticipated the cashier's question. 'I'd like a paper cover, please,' she asked, before the barcode had even been scanned.

The expert had repeated the same concept in different guises, chapter after chapter. There was no need for a total break from the previous life, but a revolution had to be set in motion. A R-E-V-O-L-U-T-I-O-N. A *revolution*! Oh God, how on earth were they supposed to do that? Coups d'état, tearing down statues of despots, throwing stones, armies in the streets: the phrase evoked only terrifying things in Yui's mind.

That winter and early spring were full of conversation: there was a lot to do. Yui and Takeshi discussed everything at length, hoping to somehow make sense of it all. From January to April they spoke of little else. It took place mostly after dinner, once Hana had gone to bed and the projected stars were flickering on her bedroom ceiling. Sitting at the clean table with a hot mug of tea in front of him, dipping the bag in and out of the water, Takeshi would voice any doubts that had come into his head and the advice he had received at the hospital from colleagues with grown-up children. Twirling a spoonful of honey in her own mug, Yui would then pose possible solutions to his questions and report back on what she had read in the manual (which had, in the meantime, tripled).

'What she should wear, for example. How do we keep her PE kit in good condition over the year and prevent it from getting worn out? Or all the gadgets that need to be attached to her rucksack: you wouldn't believe the range of things children need to be equipped with these days.'

'Seriously?' Takeshi asked, alarmed.

'Also she'll need to learn the route from home to school off by heart and try it a few times before the year starts. The best thing is to identify other children she can walk a bit of the route with. I heard there are little committees of mums who take on the task of monitoring crucial points in the neighbourhood, junctions where the children have to cross the road or turn a corner.'

'I hope they'll make do with me,' he said.

'But surely it's fine to leave that to someone who knows better than us?'

Then the night before the first day of school arrived and it was Yui, not Hana, who was too excited to sleep. 'A revolution — set in motion a revolution': the phrase spun around her head relentlessly.

Takeshi restrained himself from sending her a message in the middle of the night, but he couldn't sleep either, chewing over all the things he had preferred to keep bottled up over that long conversation from winter to spring. How would he tell the teachers about the death of his wife, and how would he explain the fact that the little girl had not uttered a word for two whole years?

Silent? Yes, silent. Completely? Yes, completely. And so on.

chapter

forty-eight

The Paper Cover Yui Chose in the Bookshop
When the Assistant Asked Whether She'd Prefer:

a) a red flower pattern with little leaves on a yellow
   background
b) a blue, dark green or red in a block colour
c) a pattern of giraffes with neckties and elephants
   with umbrellas and rubber boots in pastel colours

was b).

'Blue, dark green or red?' the shop assistant asked.

'Red,' Yui replied decisively.

chapter
forty-nine

THAT MORNING AT SEVEN THE alarm went off, and at half past seven, as promised, Yui arrived. She had covered the bags under her eyes with a thick layer of make-up and brightened her cheeks and lips with a bit of colour. When Takeshi opened the door, he found her particularly attractive and his smile was restrained, unnatural.

Yui did not notice. She sung, 'Good morning!' and hurried straight to Hana's room to help her get dressed.

They had chosen her outfit weeks ago: a blue cotton dress that fell to below the knee, open loafers with a lace and a tiny button, and a hair bobble with a little stripy bow tied around her low ponytail.

To calm their nerves they started inventing funny alternatives. 'Imagine if I burst into the classroom with a witch costume and a broom between my legs!'

'Imagine if you wore a summer *yukata* and walked around with little ballerina steps!'

The faces her new classmates would make!

Tora looked at them sideways from under the bed.

Takeshi's mother stayed in the kitchen putting away the breakfast, rubbing at plates that were already dry and repeating incredulously, 'School already, six years old, first grade!' Unsettled, she walked over to her son, squeezing his hand and touching his shoulder, as if congratulating him on that astonishing feat. 'Tora! Tora!' she then called out, offering yet another morsel of food to the kitten, who skidded into the kitchen at full speed. No matter how much weight she put on and how thick and shiny her fur became, the old woman couldn't help seeing her as a pile of bones: 'But do you feed her?' she asked. 'I mean, properly?'

'Of course we do, Mum! Please stop spoiling her or she'll be obese soon,' Takeshi reprimanded. His mother detected the worry in her son's voice (*school already, six years old, first grade!*) and didn't reply.

They sat down at the table, stomachs clenched from the excitement. Hana had requested banana special eclairs for breakfast: partly to highlight the solemnity of the occasion and partly because they had become a bit of a tradition by this point. They reiterated their promise to sit in front of the *butsudan* after school and tell Akiko, Hana's mother, all about her big day.

'Today is the start of a revolution,' Yui whispered to Takeshi as they closed the front door and the little girl, her rucksack on her shoulders and holding her grandmother's hand, was already almost halfway down the steps. Yui noticed that Takeshi was tenser than she was and that helped her to downplay the situation. Saying the words that had tormented her for months out loud at such a key moment felt liberating.

'It truly is a revolution,' Takeshi replied, taking the phrase so seriously that Yui couldn't help but burst out laughing.

251

It was only once they were on the street that Takeshi furtively hinted at his concerns about what to say to the teachers. His daughter was so delicate.

'Delicate doesn't mean fragile. Why don't you let Hana say it herself?' Yui suggested. 'Let *her* tell her story, naturally, like all the other children will.'

They crossed the first of the three alleys that separated the house from the school. The granddaughter confidently showed her grandmother the map she had drawn the previous Sunday.

'Let her tell it the way she wants to. She's been speaking normally since the visit to Bell Gardia, hasn't she?' Yui added encouragingly.

Since that miraculous day at Bell Gardia, and every day for a number of weeks, Takeshi had woken up with the fear that he wouldn't hear Hana's voice again: he would go into the kitchen and anxiously delay saying good morning to her. He smiled now, remembering how on the second day he had even pretended not to see her, terrorised by the idea that he might make a mistake that would break the spell and return her to the realm of silence. But instead Hana had behaved, without exception, just like any other child.

'People will get to know her for who she is, not for who she was,' Yui concluded, putting her index finger over her lips as they were coming up behind the little girl.

Hana's outline made Yui think of her own daughter aged two, when she had put on the penguin rucksack her grandmother had given her for the first time, her smile radiant as she twirled around the room in a fruitless attempt to see her own back, like a puppy chasing its tail.

Yui turned to Takeshi with a reassuring smile and repeated, 'Don't worry.'

In front of the school's decorated gates, under the pink clouds of cherry blossom that released showers of petals at every breath of wind, Takeshi felt convinced that Yui was right.

chapter

fifty

Hana's Drawing of the Journey from Home to School

255

chapter
fifty-one

FOR HANA IT TRULY WAS a revolution. Not just with the first day of school, but since she had started talking again, nothing and everything in her life had changed.

The frame? Yes, perhaps it was the frame that changed things. Yui was around more and more, to help with homework, she said, so that Hana's father wouldn't have to worry about staying late at the hospital. But in truth it was just because she wanted to be. And Hana loved reaching out her hand and

257

finding Yui at her fingertips. If not to the right then to the left, at exactly the same height as her father and grandmother.

The latter, though, after an early bout of enthusiasm, was overcome by jealousy. Takeshi, who knew his mother well, recognised it immediately and started inviting her to lunch more often. He would phone her on a Sunday morning – 'Why don't you pop by ours?' – or on certain afternoons when he was leaving work early and they would all go and eat a *dorayaki* or a crêpe at the stand next to the station.

It was crucial that his mother did not end up in competition with Yui. There was no way he could reprimand her at her age, and her stubbornness meant that bringing it up would only make her defensive: *Me? Jealous? Why ever would I be jealous? Do you, perhaps, think that Hana prefers her to me? Or is it you who doesn't need me anymore?*

No, that scenario had to be avoided at all costs.

Thanks to those frequent invitations and some additional attention (a cushion for her back, the brand of tofu she preferred), the old woman finally relaxed. Before going to bed or when she couldn't sleep, she would have long conversations with her dead husband in front of the *butsudan*. She would tell him in detail about that young woman who was so skinny she didn't know how she stayed upright, who wore lovely hats that made her look quite elegant, but who had slightly odd taste in shoes: always sporty and she never wore a heel. But she was kind and respectful to her and, most importantly, she seemed to make their granddaughter happy.

'She's very quiet, sometimes for so long that you begin to wonder if she's still there,' she said, polishing the *butsudan* with a rag. 'But then all of a sudden she'll speak. I swear it's always when you're least expecting it, and Takeshi and Hana stop in their tracks to listen to her. They just stand there, hanging onto her every word. You remember how distracted Takeshi can get when you're speaking to him, don't you? Well, with this woman he's like a child again. Do you remember when he used to do his homework at the kitchen table? He'd get so absorbed that even if you shouted his name he wouldn't hear you.'

The thing that most perplexed the old woman about Yui was how that same voice could flow out of the radio with such speed and confidence. She had tuned in once, out of curiosity, and was astonished: on the radio Yui was a different person entirely.

While Takeshi's mother searched for the best ways to describe the woman to her husband, Yui nested like a dove. In her own house she set up the corner of one room for Hana, where the little girl could do her homework and play whenever Yui offered to go and pick her up from school. And sometimes too she would take her along to the radio station, because Hana was fascinated by the idea of talking into a microphone. She thought it was a kind of magic that Yui could send her voice out to faraway places and reach tens of thousands of strangers, linked only through that mysterious ability to listen.

'It's like the Wind Phone, isn't it?' Hana whispered one day as Yui was tying her hair up before going into the studio. They had given Hana permission to sit next to her, as long as she promised not to make a peep.

'You speak to people, but you don't know who's listening to you. But you come into their homes and make them happy anyway.'

'I don't know about happy, but they certainly feel like they have some company.'

'Isn't that the same thing?'

Tying the girl's thin plaits in the mirror, Yui felt her eyes prickle with tears.

During that magical period, they heard that Suzuki-san had fallen ill. From then on it would only be possible to access the Wind Phone by sending an email or fax first, so that a volunteer, if there was one available, could be there to welcome them.

Just a few days later they saw the news of the tremendous typhoon that was about to hit Kujira-yama.

261

chapter

fifty-two

Extract of the Radio Programme that Takeshi's Mother Listened to Just to Hear Yui's Voice

Yui:

'. . . The way in which we, even as individuals, have introjected the idea of growth – business growth as well as individual personal growth – is something that, how can I say, it confines the

263

present to a minority status in relation to the future, which always has to be better, with more resources, more means, more instruments . . . and yet this model, which, for our listener, Matsumoto-san from Shizuoka, is capitalism in its purest form, is not . . . is not sustainable anymore. What is the answer to this? Ma'am, what is your response?'

Response of the expert (Professor Satō):

'Professor Tsubura, we have touched upon the crux of a debate that has been going on for decades in the academic world, and, well, [*putting on a voice, as if quoting*] the market will correct itself through technological innovations and the political conditions at any given time, and you can quote Professor Satō on that . . . then we would need to go into more detail on what these political conditions *will* be and what they *should* be . . . However, in general, within the capitalist model that we ourselves embody, the resources needed to meet the 2030 objectives are in fact available now, or do you . . . Are you proposing a paradigm shift?'

II

chapter

fifty-three

THE TYPHOON DESTROYED KUJIRA-YAMA. THE
wind turned the Mountain of the Whale inside
out.

The great cetacean seemed to be trying to
return to the water, to the ocean that rose up in
terrifying breakers not far below. The beast was
looking down on the world, laying claim to it in
a deafening roar.

The ground of Bell Gardia undulated in waves
before Yui's eyes.

It occurred to her that just one more step could take her to the point of no return.

The sky shattered, and as it fell, shard upon shard, Yui stretched her arms out wide. She was moving instinctively now, against all good sense. In that moment, all the voices that had been funnelled into Bell Gardia over the years surged up, enveloping her. They spun into a windmill, an unstoppable ring-o'-roses spiralling around her.

She could almost see them now, the voices, like hoops spinning wildly around children's hips.

Dead parents, lost children, missing friends and ancestors who had evaporated into history: the voices of all those who had been called by the Wind Phone were coming back to the place that had first summoned them.

Yui lost her balance and bent over to grasp the bench again. It seemed like the only stable point in that whirlwind of fury.

When she looked up, searching for the weather vane on the roof of Suzuki-san's house, she didn't find it. The sleeves of her jacket were inflated by the wind, the air polishing her body with excessive zeal.

Repeated caresses, one after the other, that gradually turn into slaps, hits and, finally, near-murderous blows. There were people who killed like that; she had read about it in a book once.

As people all over the country watched the typhoon's movements on their televisions with nervous anticipation, the storm reached its climax over Bell Gardia.

Cocooned in the plastic cover Yui had made for it, the phone box was swaying dangerously.

Earth filled the air as the wind swept up branches and leaves, and objects Yui could only guess at by size. Those ones may be roof tiles, those others garden tools. There were pots rolling around like hay bales across the vast American prairies; an abandoned plastic bag clambered up, higher and higher in the sky.

It was like watching one of those scenes filmed in space, where everything floated around, detached from the ground; the wind made it suddenly seem as if gravity was just a choice, not a scientific fact.

Everything, she thought, could come crashing down.

'It's not fair,' she mumbled. 'This place is sacred.' No one could possibly want to hurt it.

Then, at the corner of her eye, two streaks of lightning cut through the muddy brown sky. Flashing fearfully, they struck the road and disappeared.

Another two forks of light shot down, and that was when Yui started to feel scared.

The howl of the wind hurling itself into the mountainside drowned out the sound of the sea. It must be hell down there, though the dirt that filled the air made it impossible to see that far.

All of a sudden the archway over the path to the Wind Phone tilted backwards and fell. The right-hand hook of the cover, which Yui had hammered in first, was the first to come loose. She tried to move to go and put it back in, but every muscle in her body was focused on surviving the attack and not being dragged away by the gale.

Yui saw another bolt of lightning shoot to earth. A crackling sea of electricity spread across the sky, followed by a gentler sound, like an interrupted phone line; as though, somewhere faraway, a receiver was being put down, silence reigning over the room again.

Everything around Bell Gardia went dark, even the few lights that had remained on that long. The daytime on Kujira-yama and Ōtsuchi had been stolen away, and an intense darkness fell over the other side of the hill. The blackout would last hours.

Yui finally understood the risk she was taking and, perhaps because of the instinctual dread that makes all creatures fear the dark, she wished, for the first time, that she were elsewhere.

She had made a bad judgement call. 'Overestimating yourself is always a mistake,' her mother used to say. 'But underestimating yourself is far worse.'

Which one, Mummy, which one is worse?

chapter
fifty-four

Yui's Mother's Possible Response to her Question

'I've told you, dear Yui, underestimating yourself is far worse.'

(*Adding immediately afterwards:*)

'But only when you're not in any physical danger.'

chapter
fifty-five

ONCE HOPE CHANGES DIRECTION, IT loses its way and can no longer return.

Like when you pull a thread and the whole jumper unravels. Yui suddenly lost all confidence in having made the right decision. What if something happened to her? How would Hana react? Would the little girl ever forgive her for her carelessness?

And Takeshi? What about Takeshi?

She loved him. After three years she knew it. She also knew that he loved her, because he had let her know on a myriad of occasions, even when she pretended not to understand, when she would lower her eyes and buy herself time. For Yui, being ready meant knowing, and when you knew, and the other person knew that you knew, you lost the right to hide behind silence or excuses. The silence would end up speaking for itself, becoming a refusal; and although Yui was still not ready for joy, she was utterly unready for pain. Deep down, she had no intention of saying no.

But a yes, a yes spoken with conviction, was such a weighty thing. A totally different life would unfold from that point, one that wrapped the previous one up once and for all. Cardboard boxes folded closed, duct tape, into the lorry and, *Goodbye, old existence.*

She said it to herself constantly: 'You need to be certain, Yui. You *have* to be certain.' Sometimes she would start repeating it to herself in the mornings, when, along with hunger, the desire to love him was inexplicably more acute. On those days breakfast was slower, less conscious, morsels of food remaining longer in her mouth, her coffee growing cold before she brought it to her lips. She would wait in front of the television to watch a second weather forecast because she had not been concentrating the first time, flicking through the channels to find out whether to leave the washing out on the balcony or bring it inside to dry.

For Yui that was what delaying love meant, making breakfast last an hour and flicking through channels.

When the heart is ready though, it is a different matter entirely. Then you anxiously await the word, and with each day that it doesn't arrive it feels like the thing you want most is just out of reach. Like your favourite dish at the other end of a long table.

The night before, when Hana was asleep, Takeshi had finally said the words.

They were between the living room and the kitchen. He was clearing the table, laying the dishes in the sink a few at a time. Yui was putting together the little girl's *bentō* box for the next day.

'We need to buy more bags of *furikake*,' Yui said, showing him the empty plastic packaging with Anpanman on it. 'This is the last one.'

Takeshi let Hana's colourful plate and the soap slide

into the basin and straightened up slowly. A bubble floated through the air and Yui playfully blew it in Takeshi's direction.

He looked at her: 'Yui, why don't you come and live here?'

Years later, Takeshi still would not be able to explain why he had chosen that moment and not another one. He had been thinking about it for months, but kept it quiet. He had planned it out like you plan your dream house: the spacious entrance hall, the gentle slope into the living room, the bright bathroom.

He cared more though about Yui and their friendship than about anything they might become. He had planned to detect any signs of a possible refusal in advance, to never be hasty with words that were difficult to take back.

And yet.

And yet, there they had materialised, those extortionate words, between the kitchen and the living room.

Yui's long wooden chopsticks remained suspended in mid-air, holding a mince and potato croquette.

She struggled to remember where she had been putting the ingredients: the rice, the chopped strawberries, the rabbit-shaped biscuits; the strips of sticky tape for securing the sides of the *bentō* cover.

'Live here,' Yui repeated, no question. She had said this to avoid making a mistake, leaning on the echo of his words.

'You belong with us. We are a family: you, me, Hana, Tora too. All that's left is to make it official.'

He came up behind her, shielding her slim body like a cavernous seashell. In the contact between her shoulder blades and his chest, Yui had the distinct feeling that a metamorphosis was under way.

It was as if they were becoming a tree, wood and bark. Long rhizomes sprouting from their skin, followed by shoots, until they bloomed, relentlessly binding one body to the other.

This kind of change happened only once in a lifetime.

Takeshi held her tight, his face buried in her neck, repeating the phrase *Suki, Yui no koto ga suki.**

---

* I love you. Yui, I love you.

'You and Hana are the most important things in my life,' he whispered, lowering his voice another notch. 'I'm going to bed now. Sleep on it. We'll talk about it tomorrow, if you're ready.'

That was how he sealed the conversation, without even giving her a kiss.

Now Yui wondered whether that promise of immense happiness had perhaps frightened her, if it was part of the reason she had escaped in the night, heading for Bell Gardia, putting her life in the hands of the deadly typhoon.

No, she told herself: it was not fear, it was precisely the opposite. She had felt so happy to have it confirmed – she was loved, and loved in return – that she believed this love would protect her.

chapter

fifty-six

The Contents of Hana's Bentō *Prepared by Yui that Evening*

Cooked rice (of the *Koshihikari* variety).
Two florets of boiled broccoli.
Two cubes of steamed aubergine.
A button mushroom.
A mince and potato croquette.
Two pieces of *sanma* in soy sauce.

A small bag of salmon *furikake* with Akachanman on the bag.

Separate: a little banana muffin, two rabbit-shaped biscuits, six chopped strawberries, one pot of plain yoghurt.

Note: In the excitement she forgot to put the strawberries and the muffin into Hana's bag. She also broke the right ear off one of the rabbits.

chapter
fifty-seven

THE WIND CONTINUED TO BATTER the things that surrounded Yui. The fabric of the world was being dragged into the melee, like the people she always saw in Tōkyō at dawn, creased and worn out before the break of day.

And as the sky above Kujira-yama unleashed its fury upon her – and she thought that nobody else on this planet would attempt to stand up against such a sky – Yui wished she were elsewhere. Beside Takeshi, safe in his arms, with Hana's leg flopped over hers, like when they flicked through fairy tales and picture books on the sofa and they would all pile up at one end to keep warm like the monkeys in Hokkaidō, which always made the little girl laugh.

Takeshi's *arms*, Hana's *leg*.

And what if, together with that clumsy declaration of love, Takeshi had consigned her a piece of himself? What if, unknowingly, he had given her custody of a foot, a liver, an artery of his heart?

And what if Hana, squeezing Yui's hand tight when she got home from school, had secretly slipped into her palm one of her hazelnut eyes, the mole above her belly button, her rosy cheeks?

What would happen to them if Yui disappeared too?

The thought shook her. She wanted to find shelter somewhere, in Suzuki-san's outhouse, or in the old woman and her dog's shed. But it was too late. Loosening her grip would put her at risk of flying away, like the little girl with the red shoes in *The Wizard of Oz*.

As she pictured herself, ridiculous, spinning around

like a broken toy in the air before free-falling into the forest on the side of the hill or down towards the sea, Yui mused that this must be how the earth was made, everything dragged upwards. Tsunamis had to exist for a reason too. They stirred up the cosmos, just like earthquakes, floods, landslides and avalanches. All that was a disaster for mankind, all that killed, burned, drowned or displaced, protected the world's equilibrium.

Yui forced herself to consider what exactly a storm was. It was her way of making this terrifying time pass. Because in just another hour, surely, the typhoon would tire of pounding the soil at that precise point on the earth. She might find herself wounded, perhaps even bleeding in unexpected places, but she would be alive.

'I'm OK, nothing happened to me!' she would exclaim, running towards Hana and Takeshi. First she would reassure them that the pieces they had given her to look after were fine. And then she would promise to remember next time that being loved comes with enormous responsibilities, at least as enormous as those of loving.

Suddenly she heard a furious rumble of thunder. Something crashed. Yui was struck violently.

A distant whistle sounded, a mournful elegy from far away.

Soaked to the skin, held down by nothing but the ridiculous weight of her own body, Yui lay on the earth.

Her arms softened, her features became limp.

From then on she was at the mercy of the wind, her body tossed around like an empty cardboard box.

chapter
fifty-eight

Yui's Last Thought Before Passing Out

'Oh.'

chapter

fifty-nine

T HE ANTIDOTE TO POISON IS poison.

In the end it was the wind – in all its incredible fury – that saved Bell Gardia.

Word spread that the woman who went to save
the Wind Phone was instead saved by it. It became
folklore that she owed her life to the voices of the
tens of thousands of people who had gone there to
speak to their dead. Or, in fact, to the dead themselves who, even if nobody could hear them, were
responding to their living with a whisper or a caress.

291

Some people said it was both, in union with the natural presence of the wind on the hill above Ōtsuchi.

The three forces formed a wall that stood against the typhoon and protected Yui.

The area remained without water and electricity long into the evening. There was a landslide too, that brought down hundreds of pines from the forest into the valley, the rains devastating the fields on the other side of the mountain. There were houses to the west with doorways full of mud, elderly people hooked up and pulled into the sky by rescue helicopters, stretchers for those who'd had serious domestic accidents in the blackout. Hundreds of cats and dogs had been dispersed; cars were overturned by the wind; a lorry full of apples from Aomori had toppled over on the highway, scenting the road with fruit.

When Yui was found, she was surrounded by destruction.

Suzuki-san's roof had caved in, most of the tiles loosening their grip and being scattered over the vegetable garden, damaging the aubergine plants and tomato cages.

The phone box had been wrenched from its foundations and fallen over, but that wasn't what had hit Yui. On the contrary, the cabin had fallen into a protective position between her and the air filled with soil and debris that spun around above her.

She'd remained there, covered by a plastic and grass roof in a pocket of air between the bench and the cabin: it looked as though they had each offered Yui one of the plastic sheets she had wrapped them in. Thanks to those two barriers, Yui was shielded from the turmoil.

Just one more lash of wind and the phone box would have hit her, or the bench might have tipped over and crushed her head. Instead, Yui was injured, but not to the extent she should have been, given the circumstances.

It was Keita, the high-school student from the neighbouring village, who found her. He was also worried about Bell Gardia and had waited for the typhoon's most destructive phase to pass, before, faced with his father's categorical refusal to let him go alone, they travelled there together in the car.

The boy was shocked when he saw the garden. Not only by the chaos of the detritus, but because the whole thing – all the features that made up the geography of Bell Gardia and the Wind Phone – looked as though it had been caught at the centre of a spider's web, wrapped in silken thread to keep it intact, immobilised at the point of capture.

The archway had fallen, as had the phone box that now stretched out parallel to the bench, but the rest of it seemed to have held up.

Keita's father suddenly shouted, 'Hey! There's someone here! Run!' and that is how Yui was found.

She had a large haematoma on her face, a sign that something had hit her hard, but her breathing was regular, as was her heartbeat.

They gently lifted her into the car and immediately started the engine. Keita drove carefully along the road, interrupted here and there by fallen branches that they sometimes had to stop to haul aside. The wind was still strong and the thick forest that led to the hospital swayed from side to side as though drunk.

Keita's father supported Yui's head on the back seat, thinking about the best way to explain how they'd found her to the doctor at A & E, how her neck was bent, the clotting blood on her ankle, the arched position of her arm which might be dislocated. Every so often he tried to rouse her, calling her by the name his son faintly recalled: Hasegawa-san. But Yui, Keita said, was the name Suzuki-san always used.

Over the years Keita had got the impression she was a good-natured person, calm and collected, standing erect at the edge of the Bell Gardia property, from where she would look out at the ocean. She would often nibble on chocolate and always wore red.

Keita's father lowered his gaze onto Yui's skirt, which was indeed red and flared, then he took in her slim-fitting sweater, soiled with mud and leaves. Before, he had seen only the stretches and tears, not the colour.

'But what was she doing there in this weather?' the man kept asking, not believing a body as slight as this one, now battered and bruised, had managed to carry out such a titanic endeavour.

295

Yet everything at Bell Gardia had been carefully covered in sheets of plastic and duct tape, every piece secured to the earth. It must have been her; who else?

chapter
sixty

Yui's Family Name and Given Name in Full

Hasegawa 長谷川
Yui ゆい

Note: The name Yui was chosen by her mother in *hiragana* as a
wish for a 'simple and harmonious life'.

chapter

sixty-one

Yui came to Bell Gardia every month, Keita
said. She had lost her daughter and her mother
in the 2011 tsunami.

'How awful,' his father whispered and, with the
back of his hand, instinctively stroked the face of the
woman draped across his knees.

Yes, very sad, but everyone who went to Suzuki-
san's garden had a story like that. It didn't mean it
was full of miserable or depressing people. In fact,
he had met some very interesting people there.

'Have you ever met anyone who's really, *completely* happy anyway? I don't think I have.'

'I'm sure it brings her a lot of relief to be able to talk with her mother and her daughter there . . .'

Now that he thought about it, Keita had never seen her enter the telephone box.

'I'm not sure she does talk to them.'

Instead she wandered the garden, roaming up and down the rows and occasionally crouching down to touch the plants. She often went through the archway and looked up at the bell as it jingled. She observed the buds and shoots. She listened to the wind, he said.

'She hardly speaks, but when she does she says really funny things. She once confessed that, sometimes, when she thinks really hard about something, she ends up saying it out loud, without realising, and people think she's a madwoman,' Keita said, smiling.

'Your mother did that too, you know. When she was immersed in her own thoughts, sometimes she moved her lips and people would hear her. Other passengers sitting near her on the train weren't always happy about it,' the man replied, his son laughing now.

300

Keita's father knew that his relationship with his wife had been extinguished long before she died, but only like the romance between a couple who have been together for fifty years. His son, however, would not have understood the relief of loving a little less when she was torn away.

He wasn't over it by any means, but Keita's father had not suffered like many people would imagine. His guilt, however, had been flicked on like a stage light as he searched for the precise point where she had once been and no longer was.

He had sworn he would express affection for his dead wife every day, to teach his children love. Recently he had even begun to fear that he was becoming convinced by his own act, that through the fantasy he had actually fallen in love with her again.

He found himself with his heart wrung out each night, dreaming of the girl he met in the summer of his sixteenth year, on the beach they grew up on, where he had swum ashore injured but beaming over the pile of sea urchins he had collected.

The end of this sequence – her patching him up

301

and their first kiss, the only one he had ever given a woman who wasn't his mother – replayed itself night after night, unchanging.

'She must have arrived really early this morning, to do all that work,' Keita started again, unaware of his father's secret suffering. He kept thinking about Yui's astonishing task, her tenacity, despite how small she was. She was the spider that had wrapped Bell Gardia in its silky web.

'Now that I think about it, did you notice a car parked in front of the garden?' and as he finished his question Keita finally realised what had made the whole situation feel so strange: Yui was alone; Takeshi wasn't with her.

He wasn't sure how to describe that sensation to his father. It was something that was entirely feasible, but felt wrong, made everything look a little out of focus.

'She always comes with a man,' he said. 'Fujita-san. I don't think I've ever seen her without him or him without her. It's strange, they travel here together by car from Tōkyō, every time.'

'From Tōkyō? But that's so far!' Keita's father was astonished. He searched for signs of the capital on

Yui's face, of that city that swallowed up the whole of Japan and where he too, during his four years at university, had lived, suffering alternating bouts of joy and irritation at the crowds of people in the streets.

He started checking Yui's pockets, with the hesitancy of a man touching the body of an unfamiliar woman. In all the confusion, he had not thought to look for a phone. 'We absolutely must let that man know. Do you know his number?'

'Suzuki-san might, but I don't. And Suzuki-san is in hospital at the moment, remember? So I don't know how we can get it.'

'She's got nothing on her. Her bag is probably in the car with her documents. We need to go and get it.'

'I'll go back and find it. Afterwards though, while the doctors are checking her over.'

'Are you sure the man wasn't at Bell Gardia too?'

'No, at least not in the garden, otherwise I'd have seen him. Elsewhere on Kujira-yama, I don't know. We need to call him as soon as possible to make sure of that too.'

chapter

sixty-two

*(1) The Feeling (which was curiously
similar to Yui's experience of nostalgia)
Keita Had that Day and Struggled to
Describe to his Father; and (2) The Times
He Felt It Most Strongly*

1. Like something that's straight but at the same time
   imperfectly aligned. Like something that might
   seem fine when you look at it, but is a little out
   of focus, or a little to the right or the left of where

you are looking. Like something that is right in theory, but for some reason feels wrong.

2. When he saw someone finish smoking and drop the cigarette butt on the ground.

Every New Year since his mother died when the *o-sechi ryōri* tasted good, even very good, but different.

When his sister put lipstick on before going out and looked like a woman.

Every time one of them came into the house and didn't hear Mum call out, *Okaerinasai.*

chapter
sixty-three

TAKESHI DID NOT REALISE YUI had disappeared until later.

For days they had been worrying about Suzuki-san's health and talking about the emails they had exchanged with his wife. It was hard to tell how he really was, whether it was just a passing problem or something more serious.

Takeshi had seen how upset Yui was at the idea that Bell Gardia would no longer be freely accessible, that somebody who needed it might not be able to go.

That garden saved lives, she repeated over and over again; it had to be available at all times.

But wasn't that the very point of all the seminars and events that were held there? Takeshi had replied. To make people independent of the phone box, to free them of their attachment to it. If they learned to separate the idea from the place, they could create a private phone box in their own garden, or a post box into which they could put letters with no address.

It had been ten o'clock in the evening when they turned on the TV. They only meant to check the weather forecast, to find out whether to hang the washing outside tomorrow; whether they should get Hana's rubber boots out of the cupboard. Only the edge of the typhoon would pass through Tōkyō.

On the right-hand side of the screen, a man wearing a waterproof jacket, holding a yellow microphone in one hand and clutching the edge of his hood with the other, illustrated the impending typhoon with words and facial expressions. On the left-hand side, a thin presenter with a strained smile pointed his baton at a map that was covered in lines.

The contrast between the drenched correspondent and the impeccable man in the studio seemed cruel.

'Who's going to protect Bell Gardia?' Yui had asked, a hint of worry in her voice.

Unsure how best to respond, Takeshi said that even if the garden was damaged in the storm, it wouldn't take long to fix it up again; there was no need to worry. They were always saying that, weren't they? That even if it was a different telephone, in a different place, the important thing was not the object itself but what it stood for.

Yui made a vague gesture; she accepted his point, but his words didn't seem to have cheered her up. Takeshi changed the subject, talking about things they needed to get from the supermarket, then about the absurdity of his mother's obsession with mats, which she filled the house with, like the flowery doormat in the living room and the stripy ones in the bathroom. Then he began tidying up, listing his upcoming shifts at the hospital, repeating rumours he had heard about the new head physician who would be taking over in April.

As Yui was preparing Hana's *bentō*, and he was

somewhere behind her, the explosive phrase had slipped out of his mouth.

He didn't tell Yui exactly what it was he loved about her, seeing as he loved so many things. It was not just to do with Hana, though she was undoubtedly an important factor; there were, on the map of his emotions, certain paths that led back to Yui alone. The businesslike way she approached new subjects, for example; the sensual way she shook out her hair, which fell in waves down her back; the habit she had of holding on to gates and shelves with both hands; the eternally measured tone of her voice.

Although in the past he had always been attracted to curvy, bubbly women, he found himself mesmerised by the distinct lines of Yui's anatomy and her slim silhouette. Looking at her body, especially in the summer, he could trace where one piece slotted into another, where each vein began and then flowed into the next.

And yet he had told her he loved her in the most banal way possible, merely repeating one word: *suki*.★

★ *Suki* means 'I like you', and is often considered more sincere than 'I love you'.

Had he made a mistake?

She had smiled, but given no clue as to how she felt. He feared that she would resist him, which was perhaps the most likely reaction of a person who had become accustomed to having love torn away from them, who found it difficult to accept the joy that was the inevitable end to grief. But he refused to be pessimistic. No, the more he thought about it, the more he told himself he had to have faith. Love can be persuasive, given time.

He fell asleep in that state, ruminating on how, in the morning, he should demonstrate his certainty to her. Perhaps by placing his hand over her slender fingers, showing how happy he was that she was still there for breakfast. How nice it would be if every day was like this.

chapter
sixty-four

Details of the Scene Where Takeshi Declared his Love for Yui

In the background, the end credits were rolling for *In the Mood for Love* (2000) by Wong Kar-wai, one of Yui's three favourite films. Takeshi's first word fell at the exact moment the photography credits appeared on the screen.

Takeshi was wearing soft jeans from Uniqlo and a black Darth Vadar sweater. Yui was wearing a onesie with Rilakkuma on it, which had been a birthday present from Hana.

Both were barefoot.

Note 1: Yui's birthday was on 23rd June.
Note 2: *Star Wars* were Takeshi's favourite films.
Note 3: Takeshi's sweater wasn't a gift from anyone; he had bought it for himself.

chapter

sixty-five

$\mathcal{S}$OME HOURS LATER, SHIO, THE young man who always carried the Bible around with him, started his shift at the hospital. He immediately recognised Yui and Takeshi and joined them in Yui's room. It had been a while since they had seen him at Bell Gardia, and Yui and Takeshi had wondered whether something might have accidentally slipped out during his conversations with Suzuki-san. They had worried that Shio might have been avoiding them as a result, Suzuki-san's reassurances not convincing them fully.

They both knew all too well the fear of evoking pity in others, a more depressing feeling than that of pitying yourself.

However, the truth was that in recent months Shio had started to see changes in his father. He couldn't say what exactly the changes were. He was withering, it seemed. And the more signs his father showed of fading away, the more determined Shio was to watch it until its conclusion. He had not let him out of his sight for a moment; he wanted to be there when it happened.

He'd had a tenacious fever from night until morning. Nobody had dared call a doctor. He had made a point of that; that if he shouted out, they should let him be. Shio agreed: it was important not to interfere with the things that determined life.

His father had been delirious for a week, and the thing that everyone had found most extraordinary was that his body, which after the disaster had turned grey and swollen, was still able to produce such a crystalline voice, a sound that could cut through the roar of the ocean and command the waves.

In the daytime he confused the curtains in the

house for the sails of his boat, the *fusuma* sliding door for the side of the captain's cabin. Shio's aunts would enter the semi-darkness of their brother's room to bring him a tray with a light meal on it. But he didn't want to eat. If his days had once been reduced to counting down the hours to the next meal, now they were defined only by the process of weakening. 'He's killing himself,' the women whispered gravely when they went, in the evening, to collect the tray full of day-old food. 'He needs to eat or he'll die of starvation.'

But then the typhoon arrived. The wind created an infernal noise, and a pot was blown through the bathroom window, causing great commotion.

'The dead are returning,' he shouted, and everybody in the house covered their ears. It was a frightening thing to hear.

Outside, everything was creaking and screeching; it sounded like the discordant tune of a marching band, the melody disintegrating as it moved further and further away.

When the glass in the front door shattered and he heard the agitated footsteps coming and going, trying to fend off the ruinous wind, the branches and the mud, Shio's father got up to go and see what was happening. So used by now to ignoring him, nobody realised that the man had seen the truth behind the scene in front of him.

If it was the universal deluge of Genesis that had broken him, this flood was the baptism of the New Testament, which, instead of finishing him off, had roused him from his slumber.

Shio's father had begun to wail; he curled up into a ball and shook for a long time. He cried with his entire body, his eyes, his back, his throat. Nobody had seen him do that since Shio was a child and his mother had died, which felt, to his father, like the mainmast had fallen.

'He's still crying now,' Shio told Yui and Takeshi. 'Nothing can make him stop, and he keeps saying he's sorry. But he's much better; you can tell.'

Yui was lying on the bed with a thick bandage around her head and plasters on her arms, which were emerging from the sheets. Seeing her like this, calm and happy, the hospital suddenly felt like a private house, with Takeshi, standing by her side, the guest who had been invited round for tea.

'The doctor said it would be best to do some neurological checks,' Shio continued, looking at his friends. 'But he seemed quite optimistic.'

Shio had been feeling euphoric for some hours, since the moment he had sat on his father's hospital bed and leaned over his chest with a stethoscope to listen to his heart and lungs. The man had tried to stay as still as possible, but he couldn't resist the temptation to stretch his hands out towards his son's face. As if he were seeing him for the first time in years, he had whispered, 'Look how talented you are!'

Shio had fumbled with his father's shirt buttons, trying to hide his face, but as he blinked, tears fell from the corners of his eyes.

Takeshi was visibly happy for him. 'Great! Brilliant! What wonderful news, Shio!'

It had taken Takeshi a whole day to get to the hospital because of the typhoon, and in the meantime Yui had woken up and managed to recite her date of birth and Takeshi's phone number from memory. She asked what condition Bell Gardia was in, and Keita had reassured her: it would all be back to normal in just a couple of days.

Takeshi was scared to death when he had received Keita's phone call. He still could not fathom how it had turned out like this. He must have used up all of his luck in one go.

A few moments before Keita's car pulled up in front of accident and emergency, his father and Yui in the back, the typhoon had finally rolled off the land and into the sea. A tear in the thick blanket of cloud revealed an infinite expanse of blue on the other side, pouring abundant light over the earth. As the minutes passed, the opening expanded. Day had finally arrived.

Children, restless from being trapped indoors for hours, looked out of their windows and saw the clouds fleeing rapidly eastwards. The temperature rose substantially, the air became humid.

When she got home from school, unaware of the extent of the danger Yui had been in, Hana sent a message to her father saying that in Tōkyō it felt like summer again, like the evenings of *O-bon*. Takeshi replied that it was the same where he was. Out of the window, in the garden that surrounded the hospital, the last cicadas of the year resumed their deafening song.

The next day, a short while before Yui was discharged and they started the journey home, Keita and his father came to see them. They wanted to know all the details of Yui's recovery. They felt, having been on the frontline of her rescue, a duty and a right to be better informed than everyone else.

Keita's sister Naoko was with them. She was a young woman with an obstinate face and a tense jaw that let no words escape. Her father did not make the error of apologising on her behalf or of pushing her to speak, which softened the atmosphere.

And then Shio arrived, with his distinctive features, wearing a white lab coat that billowed at his sides. 'Here we come,' he announced, and the meaning behind his use of the plural materialised before their eyes, Suzuki-san appearing immediately behind him, followed by the diminutive outline of his wife.

Their voices rose in a chorus of surprise and concern: 'Suzuki-san!', 'How are you Suzuki-san?', 'But shouldn't you be resting?'

He was fine, absolutely fine; it was just a minor illness, nothing serious. They had thought it might be something much more significant, but the tests dissolved their fears. 'Just a little scare, really,' he assured them.

His wife, standing beside him, apologised at length to Yui and the others, for having made them worry. She was upset; she should have taken more time over the notice that she had written in a hurry and posted on the website. She wasn't good at that sort of thing, and she had obviously made a mistake this time.

She apologised again, struggling to hold back her emotion. Her husband put his arm around her, squeezing her tight, but she kept bowing and repeating '*Gomennasai*' and '*mōshiwakearimasen-deshita*' – 'I'm so sorry, please forgive me.'

'There is no need to apologise, really,' Takeshi interrupted. 'Yui loves that place so much she probably would have gone regardless.'

'He's right, I was reckless,' Yui agreed. 'It's nothing to

do with you, I can assure you.' She stepped closer to
the couple. 'Just imagining something happening to
Bell Gardia, to the phone box and to everything you've
built for us over the years, I was out of my mind with
worry. I'm sorry, everyone!' she said. She extended her
bow to the rest of the group.

For her, she concluded, who no longer dared ever
say anything about the future, the future had, once
again, arrived at her feet. That was the magic of Bell
Gardia.

Moved by her observation, everybody nodded,
apart from Keita's sister who, embarrassed by the
strange atmosphere that she didn't really understand,
had turned her gaze beyond the window, where
serenity now reigned.

'It's the same for him,' Keita's father said, turning
towards his son. 'He wasn't making any plans, and I
kept telling him it was strange, that at his age life
should be all about the future.' The boy nodded, but
it was clear he wanted to change the subject.

'All of us, in our own way, love Bell Gardia,' Shio
intervened. 'In the past forty-eight hours hundreds
of emails have arrived from people who have visited

the garden and were worried about the typhoon. It will take us days to respond to them all.'

Another tacit *we*, which this time enveloped everyone in the room. A room that, with so many people in it, felt as though it had shrunk.

Other patients and visitors peered in as they passed by, intrigued by the accumulation of voices. Then a nurse looked in to say that Yui was ready to go home now and politely hinted that it was time for everybody to leave.

'There really are rather too many of us,' Suzuki-san laughed. 'Either somebody needs to pop open a bottle of champagne, or we should all go home.'

chapter

sixty-six

The Brief Exchange that Yui and Takeshi
Had in the Car About Keita's Sister

'She seemed like a calm girl.'

'She was extremely embarrassed, I think.'

'Didn't she seem calm to you?'

'It's hard to say whether she was calm or not. Kids are impossible to read at that age, except when they're among other teenagers.'

'To me, teenagers represent that surrealist principle . . . what is it again . . . ?'

'Which one?'

'Wait, I can't remember. It's something like *only the incredible can be beautiful.*'

'Incredible in the sense of *extreme*?'

'Yes, everything is black or white, beautiful or revolting. Being a teenager is like that – no half measures.'

'What were you like as a teenager?'

'Like everybody else: no half measures.'

'I wonder what Hana will be like . . .'

'Like everybody else: no half measures.'

326

chapter

sixty-seven

SHIO ACCOMPANIED HIS FRIENDS TO the exit, observing their various outlines as they moved through the whirl of patients, nurses and stretchers. He followed Takeshi's right hand as it relieved Yui of her bag, as the fingers on his left hand intertwined with hers; he saw Keita's sister, Naoko, point at the remaining clouds, which had begun to slow down by that point; he alternated between waving at Suzuki-san and his wife and resting his hand by his side as the automatic doors opened and closed in front of him.

'Were they your friends?' a nurse he often had lunch with asked from behind him.

'Yes, they're people with whom I have a lot in common.'

'How nice.' She smiled. 'Are you finished here? Will you join me for something to eat?'

Shio nodded and as he fell into step beside the woman he pulled the book of Job from his pocket.

Everyone at the hospital knew about his obsession. That very nurse, after a moment of incredulity ('So you're a Christian? No? So why do you read the Bible?') had made the suggestion that he buy another copy, one that was separated into pocket-sized volumes, so that he could carry it around more easily. Now that Shio had read it once from cover to cover, he would open it at random, as if expecting a revelation.

'What does your Bible say today?' she asked him as they went through the doors into the canteen. 'Any prophecies for me?'

She wasn't teasing, just asking. She was also convinced that words, the ones you heard or read (not necessarily in the Bible, but anywhere), came to you by chance but not without reason.

She also openly admitted to voraciously reading any horoscopes she could get her hands on, even if she didn't believe in them, and the two things (astrological predictions and the Bible) were not entirely different in her mind.

'So, have you found anything good?'

'Let's see,' Shio murmured pensively. The young woman placed her handbag on one corner of the long row of tables as she waited for his response.

'Here!' Shio exclaimed. 'Listen to this.'

And he read: '*A word was secretly brought to me, my ears caught a whisper of it.*'

'Hmm, nice,' his friend said. 'Perhaps a bit too poetic for me though.'

And as she walked, in her pale pink scrubs, back towards the entrance of the canteen to look at the menu, Shio realised for the first time that *wind* was an important word in that book. It was the primordial chaos, it was what had brought the locusts to Egypt, but also what, when pushed back onto the Red Sea, had parted its waters. He recalled Elijah's meeting with the Lord in the book of 1 Kings, his journey to Mount Horeb, and the wind that—

'What are you going to have?' the nurse interrupted his thoughts. She looked at Shio's rapt face. 'Best to go with curry when you can't decide,' she said warily. 'You always know it'll be good.'

She grabbed a tray, two pairs of chopsticks and two plates of salad and set off briskly towards the curry counter.

Standing still in the middle of the hospital canteen, Shio had his revelation: there was no doubt about it, it was the phone box, the Wind Phone, that had called his father back to him, that had returned him to the world. All the breath Shio had expelled trying to speak to his dad, all those years he had spent imagining him returning to the man he was, God had channelled it all and set it aside for him.

He was suddenly sure that the same thing must happen for everyone who clambered up the Mountain of the Whale, who passed through Ōtsuchi's dark valley; for anyone who made the climb up to the blustery garden of Bell Gardia.

It was an act of pure faith to pick up the receiver, dial a number, to be answered by a wall of silence and speak anyway. Faith was the key to it all.

'Shio, come on! My curry will get cold!' the nurse said, putting the tray into his hands. 'Choose quickly! My lunch break will be over soon.'

'OK, sorry, I'll take the curry too,' he replied, pulling out his prepaid canteen card.

The wind was God's breath, he thought, as he placed the steaming plate down in front of him.

'Here's a spoon. You always forget your spoon!'

'You're right.'

Itadakimasu!

Itadakimasu!

And as they pressed their hands together in prayer and bowed their heads, Shio thought that, actually, maybe, the wind wasn't God's breath.

The wind was *actually* God.

chapter

sixty-eight

The Passage from 1 Kings that Shio Would Have Cited Had his Friend Not Interrupted Him

Then a great and powerful wind tore the mountains apart and shattered the rocks before the Lord, but the Lord was not in the wind. After the wind there was an earthquake, but the Lord was not in the earthquake. After the earthquake came a fire, but the Lord was not in the fire. And after the fire came a gentle whisper.

When Elijah heard it, he pulled his cloak over his face and went out and stood at the mouth of the cave.

Then a voice said to him, 'What are you doing here, Elijah?'

1 Kings 19:11–13

chapter

sixty-nine

THEY RETURNED TO TŌKYŌ WITH their lives in two parallel lines.

Takeshi, overwhelmed by a need for definition, tried to merge the two lines into one: they would get married; they would live under the same roof. He, Yui and Hana.

He didn't ask Yui officially, not for lack of courtesy or resolve, but because, after all they had been through, it seemed like the most natural conclusion. Everything had been leading to that point.

Yui was startled when, one Sunday afternoon, Takeshi mentioned that he thought May would be a nice month for the wedding. She tried not to let the surprise show on her face, and likewise hid her bemusement when he asked her how many guests she thought she would invite, and whether she would prefer a Japanese-style ceremony or a Western one.

Yui kept her responses vague; she mentioned that she thought registering at the city hall and having a small get-together would be enough for her. She didn't like being the centre of attention.

Wondering why that conversation had started not at the beginning, but halfway through, Yui blamed her memory. She convinced herself that she had been asked the question at some point, and that she must have just been distracted at the time. She was sure her answer was yes, anyway.

It was a yes, she was certain about that, but suddenly everything was moving so fast and she was struggling to keep up.

From Hana's reaction when she walked into the living room midway through the discussion, catching onto fragments of sentences, Yui realised that this was really big news. The little girl squeezed her tight and it was this that frightened her, far more than Takeshi flicking through the calendar in the kitchen and circling in red pen the first week of May.

In that moment, her joy was overwhelmed by distress. By a fear that she couldn't define.

Takeshi phoned her first thing in the morning because he urgently needed to talk to her about their plans for the evening. If we go to the cinema then it will be an anime, and if we have dinner, it will be *okonomiyaki*: batter all over their hands, spatulas in the air and those sprinkles of puffed rice that Hana loved so much.

But deciding what they were going to watch or eat was of course trivial. Yui had been evasive for days now, and the way she had started to subtly wriggle out of his arms, and orient every conversation (whatever the subject matter) towards an undefined future, was starting to worry him.

Two days earlier, on their way to Ginza to order the wedding rings, he had touched her shoulder on the escalator down to the metro and clearly felt Yui recoil. Later that evening she had slipped away before

Hana's bedtime story, saying she had a headache. She did the same thing the following night.

He could tell something was wrong, but whatever it was, it was clear Yui didn't want to talk about it.

Takeshi reassured himself that it was normal that she might be having cold feet; that positive changes took time too. There was no addition or subtraction in life that did not require some time for adjustment. The wedding day was edging closer, as was the move; the packing and unpacking of her old life.

Grief, Yui had once told him, is something you ingest every day, like a sandwich cut into small pieces, gently chewed and then calmly swallowed. Digestion was slow.

And so, Takeshi thought, joy must work the same way.

Yui was in the radio studio when the phone call arrived. The evening before, during the broadcast, there had been an irritating whistling sound in her earphones, but it was late and they had all decided to call it a night. But now they needed to sort it out, pulling out jacks and putting them in again, calibrating volumes, searching for the source of the problem.

The technician, bending over the sound deck that was covered in levers, controls, screens and buttons, seemed to be getting closer to the solution. 'This cable is worn out; it needs to be changed. Let's try again now.'

Yui nodded and moved back into the recording studio. It was the seventh time they had tested the earphones and she was starting to get tired.

'Now? Try speaking.'

'Testing, testing . . .'

'How is it?'

'I can't hear anything now!' she replied, relieved. 'Finally . . . it seems like it's sorted.'

As she emerged from the studio, her phone started to vibrate.

'Go ahead if you need to answer it,' said the technician, seeing her screen flashing on the counter. 'I'm going down to talk to accounts.' Yui was about to respond, but he had already disappeared with a folder in his hand.

★ ★ ★

A wedding, discreet as Yui had requested, had been arranged. Their names would be officially transcribed on the document at the city hall, while they sat on those folding chairs where they would imagine themselves together forever. The ceremony would be followed by a buffet in an Italian restaurant that you could hire for those kinds of occasions.

Perhaps Takeshi needed to know whether she had asked her colleagues if they had any dietary requirements, whether Hana's dress was ready yet, whether the necessary documents had arrived from the city hall in the district where she was born. Whether she was sad about something, and why.

But to Yui all these queries were disguising the same repetitive and stubborn question: 'Are you ready Yui? Are you *really* ready?'

The phone buzzed once more, then stopped. A notification arrived, then silence again.

She read it: 'We'll be waiting for you at 7. Hana says she still wants to eat *okonomi-yaki*. What do you say? See you later!'

She reread it: 'Yui, are you ready? Are you *really* ready for us?'

For the next few days, at the most inopportune times, an image appeared in Yui's mind of the grown-up girl that, presumably, Hana would one day become.

She had thicker and longer hair tied into a severe ponytail. In her vision, Yui would see Hana coming through the front door of the house, saying nothing, dropping her schoolbag on the floor in the hallway, and the house would suddenly be filled with echoes. She would see her wearing a high-school uniform, her legs even thinner than now, which was hard to imagine. They were certainly toned though, because she probably played tennis or lacrosse.

'How was your day?' she asked in the daydream.

Hana would reply brusquely: 'I'm tired. I don't want any dinner.'

And *bam*, her bedroom door was shut and the day was over.

Then the scene would change.

Next there was Yui who, despite not seeing herself in the frame, knew she was older. They were both in the kitchen, Yui talking about what they were having for dinner (or perhaps their weekend plans?), and Hana, with a grimace, making scornful comments, particularly towards Yui, who wasn't *real* family. Had she said something wrong? Had she criticised her? Perhaps she had denied her something? Something she really wanted.

She probably didn't deserve all that anger, but it was a matter of roles. It almost always was.

And then the backdrop would change again, the curtains sweeping back.

They were in a third place that wasn't the hallway or the kitchen. And she could hear a lecture coming out of her own mouth about homework, studying hard, taking it slow with boys, because once you've done it, it's for life – trust me, you'll never forget it – and that skirt, Hana, is pulled up too high around your waist (all teenage girls seemed to do that, so Hana would surely do it too). And that lipstick is too red, it's tacky, not right for a girl your age.

And the final scene was at Hana's bedroom door, Yui following her as she tried to escape: 'Hana, are you going out? Who with?'

'What the hell does it matter to you, Yui?'

'I'm your mother and—'

'You're not my mother. I owe you nothing!'

The truth was that: (1) even if it was Akiko there instead, it would have been no different; and (2) she would never dare to call herself Hana's mother. The idea of using that word terrified her. Almost as much as the thought of it being robbed from her again.

That was it. For days on end, all she could think about was Hana as a teenager, in battle against them, against Takeshi but especially against her. Scene after scene depicted Hana in the theoretical war that was becoming an adult. It was tough for everyone, parents as well as children; Yui could only imagine how hard it would be for her.

She remembered that even when she was pregnant, she was already asking herself how she would confront her baby's adolescence. She was terrified of that phase of development, and remembered mentioning it to the gynaecologist while, in the twelfth week of pregnancy, she examined her stomach. The doctor, looking first at the minuscule human on the screen and then at Yui's bewildered face, burst out laughing.

★ ★ ★

As she was mid-thought, the technician came back into the studio, 'Are you OK, Yui? Your face has gone pale.'

But perhaps she should have been scared of something completely different. The opposite, even: Hana would be so meek that adolescence would never materialise, that it would become no more than an unfulfilled promise. Or worse: a wasted opportunity. What if teenage Hana censored herself *because* Yui wasn't her mother? What if she held back from the total rebellion and accusation that was, in fact, essential at that age?

That would also be a disaster, and all Yui's fault, because she wasn't a *real* part of the family.

'Right, shall we do one last test?' she said, turning abruptly towards the technician. 'The whistling during yesterday's show really set my nerves on edge.'

In the week that followed, those scenes kept popping up in her mind. At the till when she had to pay for a head of lettuce and a bunch of grapes, in line for the toilets in the station, as she swiped her pass at the entrance to the radio building. She was more or less constantly assailed by the feeling that she would never be able to love Hana properly, particularly in the stormy periods.

That was what this was all about, she realised one morning as she inspected her face in the mirror. This was not about getting married, or about leaving her house. This was about becoming Hana's mother.

She remembered it had taken her around three months to fall in love with her own daughter. And she had actually given birth to her; she'd had nine months to get used to the idea. She couldn't imagine how she would feel towards a child who wasn't hers on the inevitable occasions when that child charged at her like a battering ram.

Completely wrapped up in the question of whether Hana loved her, Yui realised she had neglected the real issue.

Was she capable of loving Hana sufficiently? Would she be able to reach that level of familiarity? To scold her? To tell her, 'Now that's enough'?

chapter

seventy

The Two Worst Things Yui Thought and Felt in Those Twenty-Three Days

I loved her, but it didn't do anything. Love definitely can't save people. Love can't straighten up a garden or tidy a house. So it's not really good for anything.

Rummaging through the best memories of her daughter, her instinct was to regret having been happy. Or not having been happy enough.

chapter

seventy-one

THERE WERE LESS THAN TWO months until the wedding.

Another 11th March came and went. The anniversary became more benign as each year passed and Yui picked off the scab again to check whether the wound had healed yet.

Walking towards the entrance to Tōkyō Station, Yui saw Takeshi's number flash up on her phone screen.

They want to talk to me, she thought, but I have nothing to say.

You can always find at least one thing to say, she told herself; but she didn't feel like speaking.

Over the past few weeks she had been elusive; she'd told them she was making a new radio programme that she would be hosting and producing herself. As soon as it was finished and the first two or three episodes had aired, she said, things would be back to normal.

Yui bumped into a woman inside the station. *Excuse me*, she murmured begrudgingly; she couldn't even muster the strength to apologise sincerely. She kept her eyes down and quickened her step. When the sliding doors for the Chūō line train opened, she waited on the right-hand side. The carriage was already overflowing with people, but a few more crammed themselves in. Yui got on.

'We will soon be arriving at Kanda Station. Kanda. The doors will open on the right-hand side,' the recorded voice recited. Orderly tone, orderly words. First in Japanese, then in English.

Yui wove her way to the other side of the carriage

so that she wouldn't be in the path of the surge of people getting off.

As the train swayed from side to side before coming to a halt in line with the platform, Yui thought, once more, about the fact that she was going to become Takeshi's wife and that Hana would have her, and only her, as a mother.

Nobody else will have a right to that title. Are you sure you're up to it?

Yui could be a gloomy person. She had a tendency towards sadness; it was as if she had been born on the side of a hill and she couldn't help sliding down it.

Was she the right fit for a creature as sensitive as Hana? Wasn't she putting the little girl at risk of contracting her concealed melancholy?

A message preview on her phone showed a little teddy bear with a mouth shaped like a sideways D. It was holding a tray in its arms, with the words: *Are you coming to our house for dinner?*

She knew Hana adored the stickers in the *Line* messaging app and had a particular weakness for that series of bears. It must have been her who wrote the

351

message. When she was older, she had said on a number of occasions, she wanted to create her own virtual stickers. Was that a job?

'We will soon be arriving at Ochanomizu Station. Ochanomizu. The doors will open on the right-hand side.'

They didn't deserve her hiding from them. By the time Yui got off the train she had resolved to set things straight.

Yui took two weeks for herself. Takeshi, without realising, granted it to her.

Hana asked why. She had no idea that Yui was going through a profound crisis, or that the crisis had her at its centre. Or at least a version of her that did not yet, and might never, exist.

Yui said she had to go and request a new copy of her birth certificate from the city where she was born. In fact, the document had arrived by post days ago and was lying in a folder in her kitchen amid a mountain of other paperwork.

Usually when Yui didn't know what to do, she did nothing. Now, though, aware that time was running out and that, like in a chemical reaction, if she got the quantities wrong, she could damage everything beyond repair, she acted quickly.

Denying herself the chance to change her mind, she picked up the phone and called Suzuki-san.

'Can I come and see you?' she asked after a few minutes of small talk.

'Yui-san, you are always welcome here,' the custodian responded. He guessed from her tone that something was wrong.

'I was thinking of staying a day or two.'

'You can stay for as long as you like.'

Yui took the *Shinkansen* rather than the car this time. She wanted to have her hands free and, if necessary, to be able to close her eyes and sleep.

Before getting on the train, she went into the *konbini* to buy her usual *onigiri* and chocolate. While she was queuing up to pay she saw a woman at the photocopier. She remembered how excited her daughter used to get whenever they used the photocopy machines at Lawson or Family Mart. She loved them because while you were waiting for your copies, to help the time pass, there was a little concentration puzzle on the screen. There would be two almost identical pictures between which you had to find five differences.

For example, there would be two pictures of a rabbit carrying a basket of carrots, but one had sleeves with white stripes and one had sleeves with white and green stripes; one had a red bow on the right-hand side of its basket and the other a red bow on the left.

En route to Bell Gardia, with bossa nova playing in her earphones and an unopened magazine in her lap, Yui thought of five differences between her daughter and Hana.

After months of stopping herself whenever she was tempted to make a comparison, and perhaps thanks to the cracks that had been opening up inside her of late, she finally allowed herself to do it. She allowed herself to realise that the two little girls were both similar and different. That perhaps love made room for the possibility that she could appreciate different things about each of them.

And so, after identifying not five but ten differences

between the two girls, rather than feeling disturbed, she felt relieved.

Yui hadn't told anyone where she was really going and everyone was sensitive enough not to ask too many questions. She had told Hana she was going back to her hometown to collect some important documents and that she wouldn't have phone signal there. The girl let herself be deceived: it wasn't Yui's words that convinced her but the anxious expression on her father's face.

When Yui returned to Tōkyō, after three days in which she had been completely out of touch, she seemed happier.

She would never tell anyone where she had been, not even Takeshi; not even after they were married.

The truth was very simple: Suzuki-san had made up a little room for her on the second floor of his house, and she, like a grown-up child returning home to her parents, allowed herself to be spoilt. She slept without setting an alarm, feasted on delicious food and talked more about the future that awaited her than the past that had brought her there in the first place.

She took on some small tasks to pay her way: she held the ladder while the neighbour pruned her apple trees; she cleaned the gutter on the roof of the house and she revarnished the phone box's wooden frame. She peeled carrots and potatoes, mixed dressings, rehemmed an apron and patched a hole in a pair of work trousers.

She said nothing to Suzuki-san and his wife about her fear of becoming Hana's mother. But from the details they had heard, they understood implicitly. She said that the little girl had grown so much since starting school, she talked about Hana's two best friends, from whom she was already inseparable, and about the numerous talents she possessed; about the challenge of striking the right balance when encouraging them.

On the day she was due to return to Tōkyō, she asked for an hour to herself. It was raining. She left her bags at the doorway, walked over to the phone box and went inside.

She lifted the receiver.

For the first time, she spoke.

chapter
seventy-two

Five Points From Yui's Game of Spot the
Difference Between Hana and her Own Daughter

DIFFERENCE No. 1: *Their nails*
Hana bit her nails; there was barely any white
left after a day of school. Her own daughter, on
the other hand, loved having her nails painted;
young as she was, she knew exactly what she
wanted: alternating blue and violet polish on
each of her little fingertips.

DIFFERENCE No. 2: *Hunger*

Hana didn't eat. She was slim like Yui, who had always been too thin. It was because of her age, Takeshi said, rather than her constitution. Hana's mother had been robust and she loved the flesh on her bones; she even used to buy dresses in a larger size because she had no problem imagining herself getting bigger, adding an X to her L. Perhaps Hana would take after her; who knew? They would have to see how she developed once she was a teenager.

Yui's daughter, on the other hand, ate with an exceptional appetite. She was skinny too but in her case it was definitely her metabolism. 'I'm hungry,' she complained constantly. 'I'm soooooooo hungry.' And once she could walk (twelve months? Perhaps thirteen?), and breakfast or dinner was over, she would toddle over to the fridge, open the door with her tiny hands, and pierce the silence of the white space, imperiously demanding: 'Biscuit! Yoghurt! Carrot!'

DIFFERENCE No. 3: *Singing*

Hana never sang, yet music seemed to transport her into a state of grace. 'If she does ever sing,' Yui was certain, 'she'll sound like an angel.'

Her daughter was a tangle of melodies, each one completely divergent from the next. Despite having only a few words in her vocabulary, she would come up with lyrics, construct nonsensical phrases and be firmly convinced that she had composed the most wonderful score. 'Listen, Mama,' she would begin, and a rush of vowels and everyday words would pour out of her mouth. And Yui couldn't help but laugh.

DIFFERENCE No. 4: *Playing and Organising*

Yui's daughter arranged things by colour. Her notepads, her books and her dolls would find themselves grouped together purely because they were all white, purple or blue.

Hana valued objects for their utility. She left things where they were. It would appear that she didn't organise anything. Perhaps she did, in secret.

DIFFERENCE No. 5: *Style*

Yui's daughter was a true tomboy.

Hana was the girliest girl Yui had ever come across.

chapter

seventy-three

Yui and Takeshi often found themselves wondering *what happened next*, how people's stories were going to end. In the soft voices and minor tones that preceded putting out the bedside lamp and the descent of night, they would remind each other of the faces of the children and adults, the summer dresses, plaits and puffer jackets and all the other details of the people they had seen picking up the phone in the cabin at Bell Gardia.

Yui fondly remembered the hands of children

desperately reaching up towards the handset, like saplings hungry for light.

The two of them would write lists in their minds of the men and women shaken by grief for lost spouses. Some of them, like Takeshi, had remarried, and others had been left behind with no one to love. Wrinkled elders searching for children whose lives had been wasted in all kinds of tragedies, or for siblings they had outlived.

There was no closing act in these lives, but Yui and Takeshi custom-built sparkling futures for each of them; inventing a guarantee that life would find a way to repay them. Wishing the best for all those people was the only thing they could do.

They would diligently continue to nurture some of the relationships they had formed at Bell Gardia forever. Keita, for example. Since the young man had moved to Tōkyō to attend university, he would often come to their house for dinner and, on the ever-rarer occasions that Yui and Takeshi went to Bell Gardia, he would join them for the journey, spending the day with his father and sister before going to the phone box to update his mother on his latest achievements.

Nobody, however, heard anything more from the man who had lost his son in the rubber dinghy in the typhoon. Takeshi was disappointed. He thought often about the man's long diatribe in the tea room of Suzuki-san's house, and he felt indebted to the candour of his words for the precious conversation he and Yui had that night on the way back to Tōkyō.

One day, two years later, as she was running, out of breath, to do an interview at a cafe in Ginza, Yui saw a sign. On the shelf in the window of the independent bookshop that sold just one book each week, she read, in gold lettering: THE AGE OF IMMORTALITY.

Despite the fact that she was stressed and running late, the title pulled her in. She picked it up and, once it was clear that this book was indeed written by the man she and Takeshi had met years earlier at Bell Gardia, she bought it.

She and Takeshi flicked through the pages of the book later that evening, their minds flooding with memories of the man's secret conversations and rebukes, and the symmetry between the world of the living and the world of the dead.

'Look at this,' she said to Takeshi, and reading the scant dedication (*To Kengō, from Dad*), they would both feel moved. No more recriminations, no more 'cretin', and they would wonder whether that disjointed midnight dialogue between father and son, living and dead, was still unfolding.

When they phoned Suzuki-san to tell him, the custodian was relieved. That man hadn't been to Bell Gardia for years, but he had clearly found his own way to communicate with his son. Ultimately, that was what he wished for everyone who came there – that each person would find a place where they could tend to their pain and heal their wounds. That place would be different for each one of them.

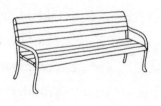

chapter

seventy-four

*The Address of the Tōkyō Bookshop Yui
Passed that Day*

Morioka Shoten & Co.
1-28-15 Ginza, Chūō-ku, Tōkyō
1st floor, Suzuki Building

Epilogue

YUI HAD TWO DAYTIME PROGRAMMES on the radio now. She had given up working evenings, because she loved their family dinnertimes so much. She, Takeshi and Hana would talk about their days and, after the wedding, Takeshi's mother joined them more often too.

Yui found the rapid-fire questions her mother-in-law welcomed her home with irritating and, like Akiko, her loquacity somewhat excessive. But she didn't let it bother her. In fact, Yui was grateful;

she seemed to have lost her knack for conversation outside the radio studio. She loved to be quiet, floating at the edges of the house, watching the knot of warmth and beauty that pulsated in its centre: Hana and Takeshi, and she herself, in the wonderfully repetitive daily scenes that unravelled in the living room, kitchen or bedroom.

When those faces she had come to love showed signs of weariness and retreat, she would caress them with even more affection. Yui loved how people looked when they were drained of energy, but when she told people that, they didn't believe her. They seemed to take it as a backhanded compliment: 'You look tired, but you don't look bad.' It really irked some people. But Yui was being sincere; she found tired faces fascinating. Sometimes she wondered whether this had originated during those early-morning meetings at the Shibuya Crossing: Takeshi's face was always still crumpled up from sleep, and that's how she fell in love with him.

Her new child, the one that would soon be growing inside her, the baby that on that first visit to Bell

Gardia Yui could never have imagined in her wildest dreams, would only discover his mother's love of fragility once he had grown up. She had seen it, stripped bare, as plain as a dictionary definition, in the people around her.

It had started during the month she spent, her soul in shreds, in that school gymnasium that clung to the mountainside with a view of the sea. Not any sea, but an ocean that had washed far onto the earth and then retreated again.

Yui had come to know fragility mostly inside herself, in every crack that appeared over those interminable years, from March 2011 to the day she met Takeshi, then to the day she finally picked up the receiver of the Wind Phone and talked to her mother and daughter again.

Yui didn't like to talk about her own frailty. But in the end she had accepted it, and that was the start of her path towards taking care of herself again. Acknowledging it helped her connect to the truest part of other people; it was what made it possible to feel close to them, part of their lives.

If someone were to ask her now, she would have

explained it with great conviction: life decays, countless cracks form over time. But it was those very cracks, the fragility, that determined a person's story; that made them want to keep going, to find out what happens next.

A day would come when Yui would cry and those tears would be both a baptism and a funeral. A beginning and an end.

They would be in Yokohama Station, taking Hana and her one-year-old brother to the Anpanman Museum, and the little boy would be wearing his *Shinkansen* rucksack, the pink and emerald-green train that served north-east Japan. The toddler would suddenly wriggle out of Takeshi's arms, where he had been carried until that point, and toddle towards the descending escalators, which he loved almost as much as he feared the ones coming up.

And as the train going in the opposite direction pulled into the station, the little boy catapulted himself into the bench that everybody was hurrying to get up from and screamed, 'Maaamaaa!' The clarity of his voice would leave all three of them dumbstruck.

That day, without warning, Yui had been reinstated with the title. It was the first time their son had called her 'Mum'.

Yui froze, her bottle of green tea in one hand and Hana's small fingers in the other.

'What? What did he just say?' she would ask her husband as a throng of Chinese tourists wrapped around them like a scarf.

'He said *mama.*'

And there it was. The latest in a series of astonishing banalities; the best one of them all.

In the midst of the commotion of the station, against the backdrop of the disciplined voice repeating directions, arrivals, departures and exits, they would stand in silence, honouring what had just happened.

Acrobatically scooping up his son in one arm, Takeshi would embrace Yui with the other. And soon the word would become contagious, just as his mother had predicted. Because Hana would have caught onto its power, and she too would start calling her *Mum*, *Mummy*, *Mama*, and would repeat it excitedly, like a magic spell.

After years of calling her 'Yui' or 'Yui-*chan*', 'Mama' finally arrived, and from then on the three words would be interchanged at random.

That was where joy was born. It resided in a re-instated word that would always remind her of the *before*, and solidify the *after*. Just like the wind that was being created there, right where they stood, between the two trains that glided into Yokohama Station and accelerated out again, pulling in two directions at once.

Everything always came back; it just needed to be called by the right name.

Was it possible that such vastly different feelings could reside within the boundaries of a single word? Could that word be used with one emotion, without the other trailing behind it like a tail?

No, it probably couldn't, just like they couldn't give Hana chocolate without her entire outfit ending up covered in it, or like their little boy couldn't learn to walk without a baffling number of bruises appearing all over his body.

The word needed to be reinforced, to be made

into a name that she could be called repeatedly, even thirty times in an hour.

Yui came to understand that there was always joy somewhere within unhappiness. That inside each of us we preserve the fingerprints of those who taught us how to love, how to be both happy and unhappy in equal measure; of those who explained how to differentiate between feelings and how to navigate the overlap, the areas that make us suffer, but that also make us different. Different and special.

That evening, and over the years that were yet to come, Takeshi would reveal that he understood this too:

'The more I move forward, the more I find myself sure,' he would say, 'that we are all fixed at the moment of our first word.'

Yui's first words into the Wind Phone

'Hello?'

'It's Yui.'

'Mum, it's Yui.'

Yui's second words into the Wind Phone

'Hello?'

'Sachiko?'

'I'm here, it's Mummy.'

Referenced Works

Foenkinos, David, *La délicatesse* [Delicacy], Paris: Gallimard, 2009.

Itaru, Sasaki, 風の電話:大震災から6年、風の電話を通して見えること [Six Years on from the Great East Japan Earthquake: what we can see through the Wind Phone], Tōkyō: Kazama Shobō, 2017.

Itaru, Sasaki and Yuriko Yanaga,「風の電話」とグリーフケア: こころに寄り添うケアについて ['The Wind Phone' and Grief Care: looking after the heart], Tōkyō: Kazama Shobō, 2018.

An Important Note

THE WIND PHONE IS NOT a tourist destination. Don't look for it on a map. Don't try to find Kujira-yama unless you intend to pick up that heavy receiver and talk to somebody you have lost.

Don't go there with a camera around your neck, don't bring out your phone, instead hold your heart close. Caress it as you proceed along the path that leads to the phone box; reassure it that everything is OK. Allow it to open up.

★ ★ ★

There are places in the world that must continue to exist, beyond our experience of them. Like the Amazon rainforest, or Selinunte in Sicily, or the sculptures of Easter Island. Places that must remain, whether we visit them in our lifetimes or not. Bell Gardia is one of those places.

I personally experienced profound hesitation about going there. I justified not going for years by saying I had too much work on, it was too far from Tōkyō, that the area damaged by the 2011 disaster was too hard to access. I even blamed it on pregnancies, breastfeeding, and tiny children running around. The truth is that I was afraid of taking something, of stealing time and space from someone who needed it more than I did.

While writing this book, I understood how important it is to write about hope. The task of literature is to suggest new ways of being in the world, to connect the *here* to the *there*. For me, the Wind Phone is mainly this: a metaphor that suggests how precious it is to hold on tight to joy as well as pain. That even when we are confronted by the subtractions, the things that life takes from us, we have to open ourselves up to the many additions it can offer too.

Sasaki Itaru and his wife manage the garden of Bell Gardia alone. If you would like to support the existence of this wonderful place and the charitable foundation that the Wind Phone depends on, which also organises many activities throughout the year to support the area and those who live there, take a look at the official website:

http://bell-gardia.jp/about_en.

There you will find out how to donate.

Acknowledgements

THIS BOOK CAME INTO THE world thanks to the wonder that is the Wind Phone and to Sasaki Itaru and his wife who conceived of and generously shared it with everybody who needed, and still needs, such a place. The figure of the custodian in this book is only loosely based on him, just as the setting of Bell Gardia is the inevitable fruit of my personal impressions. I suspect that the intrinsic spirituality of the place means that it appears differently to each person who comes to know it.

I decided to keep the garden's name as homage to

the tireless work and enormous heart of the Sasakis, and in the hope that Bell Gardia will be imprinted on our collective memory as one of the world's strongest sites of resilience.

Bell Gardia has been transformed into a magical place, profoundly imbued with spirituality, by the people who have visited it over the years. Its story is the product of a large community of individuals and families who have experienced grief. Therefore, I hereby acknowledge and thank them.

The form that this novel has taken is largely thanks to Cristina Banella and Laura Sammartino, my dearest friends. Laura, thank you for the title (the original Italian title is *Quel che affidiamo al vento*, which translates as 'What We Entrust to the Wind'). Thank you to Maria Cristina Guerra, tireless and always there, for believing in this story from the very first moment, and Francesca Lang, whose evident trust moves me every time I encounter it. A special thanks to Laura Buonocore, who saw the story's depth, and to Pina, who showed it so much love. Diego, my heartfelt thanks to you too.

In the alphabet of affection there is always my family. All of you. From the roots to the tips. Special thoughts go to Mario di Giulia, and to Franca's luminous memory. For the love that, when it's as intense as this, is destined to last.

If it weren't for my beloved parents-in-law, Yōko and Yōsuke Imai, I would never have found the time to write this novel. My debt of recognition for you is infinite.

Thank you to Ikegami Sakura, Matsubara Ayumi and Kyōko Fukawa, for providing the atmosphere of a public yet private space, where I was able to write this novel for an incalculable number of hours. For a similar reason, my sincere thanks to Kawase Reiko, Miura Yuki, Saitō Momoko and Shimamoto Terumi. And above all to Sasakawa Nanoka, for the precious documents you provided about the tsunami that hit your community in 2011.

It is a rare thing to be able to thank those who have contributed to bringing a book abroad, but *Quel che affidiamo al vento* enjoyed an extraordinary amount of attention in the months before its publication. And so I would like to express my deepest gratitude to

Luisa Rovetta and all of the wonderful staff at Grandi&Associati. Thank you to Cristina De Stefano, Viktoria von Schirach, Caterina Zaccaroni, Tomaso Bianciardi and many, many others, who took this book by the hand and led it around the world. I would like to warmly thank Antony Shugaar for translating that first extract that set so many wheels in motion.

For the English edition, I would like to thank Sophie Orme and Ilaria Tarasconi for deciding to publish my book and Lucy Rand for having reformulated it so carefully in a distant tongue. I am so happy that this novel is coming out in the UK, a country for which I have a long-held affection.

In the wake of the Tōhoku disaster, the world's media zoomed in on the nuclear fallout at Fukushima and its political and environmental implications. This book intentionally does not make reference to this and is dedicated instead to the victims of the tsunami of 11th March 2011.

Reading Group Questions

1. 'Everybody's grief looked the same at first but, ultimately, was unique.' How do the various characters within the novel deal with grief differently?

2. How does the novel look at memory, and how do Yui and Takeshi's ways of remembering the lost differ?

3. Do you see *The Phone Box at the Edge of the World* as a love story?

4. Yui and Takeshi meet many other characters at Bell Gardia. Who was your favourite?

5. Why do you think Yui risks her life to save the phone box?

6. Why do you think it takes Yui so long to speak into the Wind Phone?

7. What role does food play in the book? How does it help Yui and Hana bond?

8. Why do you think the man with the blue photo frame chooses to look at the world through it? How does it help him?

9. Yui's name means 'simple and harmonious life'. What role do names play in this novel?

10. Yui at times feels guilty for being happy after her daughter and mother's deaths. How does this affect her relationship with Takeshi and Hana?

11. Why do you think Hana chooses not to speak? How does the Wind Phone help her start again?

12. How does the novel explore family, and what it means to be part of a family?

13. What did you think of the structure of the book? What is the significance of the lists and other elements throughout?

14. Do you think *The Phone Box at the Edge of the World* is more about grief, or about hope?

**'Stories are what connect us, and remind
us that hope is always possible'
Heather Morris**

Sharing stories brings us together
They connect us to each other
They remind us of what truly matters
And bring us hope when we need it most

HEATHER
MORRIS

bestselling author of
The Tattooist of Auschwitz and *Cilka's Journey*

Coming September 2020

Find out more:
www.heathermorrisauthor.com
www.yourstoriesofhope.com
www.facebook.com/HeatherKMorrisAuthor

Glossary

Akkanbe! Bero bero be! あっかんベー！ベロベロベー！
Akkanbe describes the gesture of pulling down
one eyelid and sticking one's tongue out. *Bero
bero* is an onomatopoeia that describes wiggling
one's tongue.

Anpanman アンパンマン Very popular cartoon
featuring a superhero with a bread roll filled
with bean paste for a head.

Azuki 小豆 Reddish-brown bean often boiled
with sugar and made into a paste called *an*. It is
used in many Japanese sweets and desserts.

Bentō 弁当 A packed meal in a box, typically carefully prepared by Japanese housewives for their husbands and children.

Boshi techō 母子手帳 Abbreviation of the term *boshi kenkō techō*, meaning 'mother and child health handbook', in which mothers record the various phases of pregnancy, the development of the fetus, the baby's vaccinations, etc.

Butsudan 仏壇 Buddhist household altar found in many Japanese homes, usually in the form of a platform or cabinet, used to honour deceased family members.

-chan 〜ちゃん Affectionate informal name-ender, mostly used for females, as well as for babies, young children and grandparents.

Chirashi-zushi ちらし寿司 Meaning 'scattered sushi', *chirashi-zushi* is a dish that consists of a bowl of sushi rice covered in a variety of ingredients including fish, vegetables, strips of omelette and dried seaweed. It is often eaten on *Hina-matsuri*.

Chōchin 提灯 Lanterns traditionally made from a bamboo frame and sheets of rice paper hand-painted with designs and patterns.

392

Dorayaki どら焼き *A* pancake filled with *azuki*-bean paste.

Edamame 枝豆 Young green soy beans, cooked and eaten as a snack.

Ema 絵馬 Decorated votive wooden plaques sold at shrines. The purchaser writes a prayer or gratitude for a granted wish and hangs the plaque at the designated place in the shrine.

Family Mart ファミリーマート One of the three large convenience-store franchise chains in Japan.

Furikake ふりかけ A dry seasoning often made of flakes of dried fish, seaweed, sesame seeds and salt, usually sprinkled over white rice. It is packaged in individual bags or jars.

Fūsen-kazura 風船葛 'Balloon plant' (*cardiospermum halicacabum*), a vine with bell-shaped fruits.

Fusuma 襖 Vertical rectangular panels that can slide and be removed to divide the spaces inside a traditional Japanese house.

Gaman-du yoi 我慢強い Very patient, persevering.

Geta 下駄 Traditional Japanese sandals made of an elevated wooden base with a fabric thong. Worn with *yukata*.

Gomennasai ごめんなさい 'I'm sorry'.

Higan-bana 彼岸花 The red spider lily (*lycoris radiata*), often known as the flower of the dead.

Hiragana 平仮名 The characters that, together with *kanji* and *katakana*, make up the Japanese writing system.

Hina-matsuri ひな祭り 'Doll's Day' or 'Girls' Day' is a festival celebrated every year on 3rd March, during which a set of ornamental dolls representing the Imperial Court is displayed on a tiered platform.

Hōjicha ほうじ茶 A variety of roasted green tea.

Itadakimasu いただきます Said before a meal while bringing one's hands together and bowing slightly.

Itterasshai 行ってらっしゃい Literally meaning 'please go and come back', this phrase is used to say goodbye to somebody who will soon return. Usually accompanied by *ittekimasu*, said by the person leaving, meaning 'I'm going but I'll be back soon.'

Izoku 遺族 Bereaved family, or those left behind.

Jan ken ジャンケン Rock, paper, scissors. Used to

settle all manner of disputes in Japan, by adults and children alike.

Juku 塾 Privately run tutoring or 'cram school' to help school students with their schoolwork and exam preparation.

Kanji 漢字 The ideographic characters originating from Chinese that, together with *hiragana* and *katakana*, make up the Japanese writing system.

Kan kan カンカン Onomatopoeia that describes the sound of the bell at a level crossing.

Katakana カタカナ The characters that, together with *kanji* and *hiragana*, make up the Japanese writing system. Mostly used for foreign loan words and emphasis.

Kaze no denwa 風の電話 The Wind Phone

Kazoku 家族 'Family'.

Kendō 剣道 A martial art that uses bamboo swords.

Kimono 着物 Traditional Japanese dress worn by both men and women. Nowadays used only for very formal occasions such as weddings and funerals.

Konbini コンビニ Convenience stores open 24 hours a day, 365 days a year.

Koshihikari こしひかり A popular variety of Japonica rice.

Kujira-yama 鯨山 The Mountain of the Whale

-kun 〜くん Informal name-ender most commonly used for boys, male teenagers and between adult male friends.

Lawson ローソン One of the three large convenience store franchise chains in Japan.

Line ライン The most popular instant-messaging app in Japan.

Manjū 饅頭 A traditional Japanese sweet, often a pastry-like shell filled with *azuki*-bean paste.

Melon pan メロンパン A sweet bread covered in a crisp crust, very popular in Japan.

Miko 巫女 Shrine maiden – the young woman who assists in a Shinto shrine.

Mochi もち A paste made from steamed rice that has been pounded until it has an elastic consistency. Eaten alongside Japanese meals, in soups, and used in many traditional sweets.

Momiji 紅葉 Japanese maple tree, the leaves of which turn bright red in autumn.

Mōshiwakearimasen-deshita 申し訳ありませんでし

た Very formal apology.

Nagatsuki 長月 Meaning 'month of long nights', *Nagatsuki* is an old name for September, from the ancient lunar calendar.

Namazu なまず In Japanese mythology, a giant catfish that causes earthquakes.

NHK Stands for *Nippon Hōsō Kyōkai*, Japan's national broadcasting corporation.

Nyan nyan ニャンニャン Onomatopoeia that describes the sound cats make, equivalent to the English 'miaow'.

Obi 帯 A sash for *kimonos*, made from thick and rigid fabric and tied around the waist.

O-bon お盆 Buddhist summer festival to commemorate the dead.

O-hagi お萩 Traditional Japanese sweet made from *mochi* coated in *azuki*-bean paste.

Ohayō-gozaimasu おはようございます Greeting used in the morning. Shortened to *Ohayō*.

Okaerinasai お帰りなさい Phrase used to welcome somebody back. It is usually accompanied by the phrase *tadaima*, said by the person returning.

Okonomi-yaki お好み焼き Japanese savoury pancake.

Omiyage お土産 Gift or souvenir brought back for colleagues, friends and family after a trip.

Onigiri おにぎり Rice ball usually made from white rice and often covered in *nori* seaweed and filled with salty, sweet or pickled fish or vegetables.

O-sechi-ryōri おせち料理 Typical food eaten at New Year in Japan. It is made at home or ordered in and comes in colourful stacked boxes. Each item is believed to have a particular significance, such as bringing fortune or a long life.

Otōsan お父さん 'Father'.

Otsukaresama-deshita お疲れ様でした Phrase used at the end of the working day, to thank somebody for the work they have done, or to acknowledge the end of a group or individual task. The phrase literally means 'you have worked hard'.

Pachinko パチンコ A popular form of gambling involving slot machines and pinballs. *Pachinko* parlours are widespread in Japan.

Rakugo 落語 A form of storytelling, often comical, performed as entertainment.

Rilakkuma リラックマ Rilakkuma is a fictional lazy

bear character, popular with both children and adults.

-san 〜さん Respectful name-ender used for people of any age and any gender.

Sanma さんま Pacific saury (fish), a popular autumnal food in Japanese cuisine.

Senbei せんべい Rice crackers in various shapes, sizes and flavours. Usually savoury but sometimes sweet.

Shichi-go-san 七五三 Festival held in Shinto shrines on 15th November to celebrate girls aged three and seven, and boys aged five and, less commonly, three.

Shinkansen 新幹線 High-speed bullet trains operating all over Japan.

Shio 塩 'Salt'.

Sukiyaki すき焼き A hotpot-style shared meal consisting of beef, tofu, green onions and mixed vegetables cooked at the table in a soy-sauce broth.

Sumimasen すみません 'Excuse me' or 'sorry'.

Tanuki 狸 Japanese raccoon dog. *Tanuki* statues are found outside many restaurants, shops and bars in Japan as they are believed to bring good fortune and generous customers.

Tatami 畳 A mat covered in woven straw used as flooring in traditional Japanese rooms.

Tōdai 東大 Abbreviation of the famous University of Tōkyō, *Tōkyō Daigaku*.

Torii 鳥居 Large gate usually found at the entrance to Shinto shrines.

Ukiyo-e 浮世絵 A genre of Japanese art from the 1600s to the 1800s that includes woodblock prints. Many prints from this period are iconic today.

Yukata 浴衣 A lighter, more casual version of the *kimono*. Traditionally worn as a bathrobe when staying at a hot-spring resort, but now often worn for summer festivals and events such as firework displays.

Yukue fumei 行方不明 Meaning 'whereabouts unknown', used to describe the bodies that have not yet been found after natural disasters.

Zabuton 座布団 A cushion used when sitting on the floor.